SEP 25 2015

Withdrawn/ABCL

D0117980

3 9075 04991970 4

Best *of* Breed

THE BICHON FRISÉ

Guide
opy To
or Dog

Generously Donated By

Richard A. Freedman Trust

Albuquerque / Bernalillo County
Libraries

Edited By
Chris Wyatt

ACKNOWLEDGEMENTS

The publishers would like to thank the following for help with photography: Chris Wyatt (Bobander); Pauline Johns (Manoir); Mike Beater; Emma Roche (Rassau); Phil Shepherd (Calpastor); Karen Graeber (Whitebred); Hearing Dogs for Deaf People; Pets As Therapy.

Cover photo: © Tracy Morgan Animal Photography (www.animalphotographer.co.uk)
Dog featured is Fiyero Hillbilly Rock at Bobander, owned by Chris Wyatt.

page 9 & 31 © The K9 Breed Bar Photography/Steve Jefford; page 9 © John Hartley;
page 53 © istockphoto.com/Ana Abejon; page 74 & 110 © Carol Ann Johnson;
page 62 © istockphoto.com/Vitali Parfonov; page 82 © istockphoto.com/Gary Martin;
page 110 (top) © Carol Ann Johnson; page 110 (bottom) © Ashby Photography.

The British Breed Standard reproduced in Chapter 7 is the copyright of the Kennel Club and published with the club's kind permission. Extracts from the American Breed Standard are reproduced by kind permission of the American Kennel Club.

THE QUESTION OF GENDER
**The 'he' pronoun is used throughout this book instead of the rather impersonal 'it',
but no gender bias is intended.**

First published in 2010 by The Pet Book Publishing Company Limited
St Martin's Farm, Zeals, BA12 6NZ, UK.
Reprinted in 2012 and 2015 by The Pet Book Publishing Company Limited.

© 2010 Pet Book Publishing Company Limited.

All rights reserved
No part of this book may be reproduced or transmitted in any form or by any means, electronic or mechanical, including photocopying, recording, or by any information storage and retrieval system,
without permission in writing from the publisher.

ISBN
978-1-910488-11-9
1-910488-11-9

Printed by Printworks Global Ltd., London/Hong Kong

CONTENTS

GETTING TO KNOW THE BICHON FRISÉ

Chapter 1

The Bichon Frisé is a most delightful little Toy dog whose only purpose in life as a companion dog, is to bring joy and love to his owner. His endearing character has made him one of the most successful and popular little dogs in modern times, and because of his distinctive appearance and happy agreeable nature, he is proving to be a very suitable addition to many families.

As a clown-like dog which entertained, the breed was first recorded as being very popular with the early sailors who sailed around the Mediterranean sea trading their goods from one port another. The sailors kept the little dogs for their own amusement and also traded them as their popularity spread. They were originally called, 'Bichon Tenerife' as it was specifically on the island of Tenerife, which is one of the Canary Islands off the coast of Africa, where the breed first became established.

Breeders in Belgium developed the breed in between the two World Wars and it soon made its way to France. In 1934 it became established as a breed that was to be recognised and exhibited as a pedigree dog and was granted recognition by the Federation Cynologique Internationale. It has always been recognised as a French breed and this is reflected in its name the Bichon Frisé (pronounced bee-shon free-zay) which means curly-coated dog

PHYSICAL CHARACTERISTICS

The Bichon is a small toy dog with a size range of anything between 9 and 11 inches (23-28 cm) when measured from the withers, which is the highest point of the shoulders. A Bichon can weigh between 10 and 14 lbs (5-6 kgs) depending upon height. But he should always be small enough to carry around tucked under your arm – although many Bichons will be too lively to want to do this!

The ideal stature of a Bichon could be described as being a little more well-bodied than a Poodle but not as chunky as a West Highland White Terrier. He should be somewhere in between with a firm, well-rounded body with substance and well-defined muscle. He is a tough little dog who can rough and tumble with an active family one day yet still have all the elegance and glamour that we expect to see in the show ring.

The Bichon's size is suitable for just about any requirement that might be sought when looking for the ideal pet. Not too big which could present a problem to the elderly or to small

The Bichon is a dog of substance who can stand a fair amount of rough and tumble

children, and not so small that he would be in danger of being trampled or harmed living amid the hurly busy of a busy, lively family. In fact, the Bichon is one of the most adaptable breeds I know, happy to be a lap dog, living a quiet, sedentary life with an older family, or playing the lively clown with a younger, more active family.

THE BICHON COAT
The Bichon's outstanding feature is his soft, curly, beautifully white coat, which gives him a very round and cuddly toy-like appearance. Bichons are only ever white, so beware, if you are offered a dog described as being a Bichon and he is not white as he is unlikely to be pure bred.

The unusual coat is what distinguishes the Bichon Frisé from any other breed; there is no other coat quite like it. It is a plush coat of long hair, which has the appearance of a corkscrew, which when blow-dried, will contribute to its powderpuff appearance. In its natural state, the coat is curly, quite long and very soft to the touch. There should be no wiry or coarse hair in the coat; it should feel very soft and luxurious.

There are a number of minor variations to the coat; some are curlier than others, some are slightly harsher. Regarding coat, 'the thicker, the better' is the aim of the breeder, although this is not the easiest coat to look after. The coat changes slightly from season to season and will become thinner and sparser as the dog becomes older.

THE WORKLOAD
Keeping the coat white and clean is all part of the joy of owning a Bichon. If you hate the thought of bathing and grooming, a Bichon is not the breed for you. A Bichon needs to be bathed at the very least once a month, but this depends on how you exercise your dog. Long walks in the woods and across muddy fields can take their toll on any coat and more regular bathing may be needed. If your lifestyle is gentler with quiet walks in the park on the pathways, your dog will hardly become soiled at all.

Regular grooming is essential, but deciding on just how often this will be necessary will depend upon your lifestyle. If you do not

The superb coat is a Bichon's crowning glory – but think about the workload...

Photo: Steve Jefford (The K9 Breed Bar Photography)

look after the coat, it will mat and tangle so badly that the only option will be to have the coat shaved off at a grooming parlour. If you are keeping your Bichon as a pet you can expect to bath him around once a fortnight and give him a good brush and comb through at least every third day.

Many breeders will advocate daily grooming, but, personally, I have found this unnecessary, although most dogs really enjoy the attention. If the dog is groomed properly each time then the attentive owner will soon come to know how much work is needed to keep the coat in good order. The quality of the coat can vary considerably; a daily groom may be required for one type of coat but a weekly session could be more than enough for another.

If the coat is washed, brushed and combed, but not trimmed, the hair will become longer and longer. It will then appear to stop growing in length but become very big and bushy and very difficult to maintain. Trimming at some level is necessary and absolutely essential around the face if your dog is going to be able to see where he is going.

Whether you choose to have your dog professionally trimmed, or you decide to keep him tidied up yourself, it is necessary to keep the coat at a manageable length for the dog's own comfort. Beneath a long, bushy coat, mats can easily form and sore spots, debris and parasites can remain undiscovered. If you choose to have your dog professionally trimmed, this will need to be done every four to six weeks depending on how quickly your dog's coat grows and how well you cope with regular brushing.

In the show ring, the Bichon is presented to a very high standard, and this requires a huge amount of dedication and

Presentation in the show ring has reached new heights.

hard work. To keep a Bichon in a 'show coat', the coat has to be protected from staining and damage if the pure-white sculptured outline is to be maintained throughout the show season. Keeping the balance between not allowing the coat to be stained by food or urine, yet still allowing the dog to lead a normal life with walks in the park and playing roughly with kennel mates requires hard work and dedication by the exhibitor. This can be achieved, but it can present you with many problems. Watching your beautiful, white show dog chasing around a field with a puppy close behind and catching hold of his beautiful tail in the throws of a great game can provide joy and horror at the same time for the exhibitor. It

provides excellent exercise and helps with muscle building – and it is certainly great fun for both dogs – but it can result in coat damage and risk injury.

On average, a show dog needs considerably more grooming because the coat has to be preserved, especially in areas such as the hocks, tail and head where the coat is expected to carry more length. Frequent bathing is required because urine stains cannot be washed out if they have remained in the coat long enough to dry. Areas such as the corners of the eyes and around the mouth may need daily washing if your show dog is prone to staining on these areas. Sometimes the face furnishings are wrapped up to protect them, such is the importance of

presenting a pure-white coat in the show ring.

TRIMMING

Trimming a show dog requires expertise that can be learned with practice and, for many exhibitors, it can provide much enjoyment and satisfaction. Scissoring the mature coat, which has been carefully washed and blow dried into the powderpuff shape, provides a blank canvas for the groomer to work his magic. To carefully sculpt around the required outline, following the natural contours of the dog, perhaps leaving the hair a bit longer down the front of the legs, cutting around the curve of the legs and shaping down the chest, and finishing with rounding off the beautiful shape around the head, can be very satisfying indeed. Unlike most other breeds, the finished appearance of the show Bichon is very dependent upon a high level of presentation.

THE BICHON HEAD

The Bichon has a very even featured prettiness to his face, which is the result of the essential equilateral triangle that can be visualised between the outside corners of the eyes and the tip of his black nose. If the nose is longer than this line, or his eyes set too close together, the balance is lost and the face is never quite as pretty.

The eyes should be round, not too small nor too large, but big enough to be in balance with the overall size of his head. In

ALLERGY SUFFERERS

One of the biggest advantages – and often one of the main reasons why a Bichon is the dog of choice – is his type of coat. Because the coat does not shed in the same way as most breeds, it is less likely to be a problem to those people who suffer from allergies or asthma. It would be wise, of course, if you are a sufferer, to try to spend some time with the breed before you buy a puppy. Many breeders who understand such problems, will give you the opportunity to do this.

There is nothing worse and more upsetting than to bring your new puppy home and then discover one of the children is sensitive to the coat.

Another advantage is that Bichons do not smell in the same way as other breeds with shorter coats. They do not have the typical, wet-dog smell because they do not produce the same oils in their coats, and the oils they do produce are washed out regularly. This can be a massive bonus if you keep a number of dogs together.

comparison, a Chihuahua has eyes that are relatively large for the overall size of his face, and a Bull Terrier's eyes appear almost too small for his face. It is a matter of balance.

The colour of the eyes should always be fairly dark. They should never be amber or even light brown; the correct shade is medium brown through to black. The rule is: the darker, the better but, more importantly, the eyes should have that mischievous twinkle that says: "I'm ready to play".

A Bichon's skin pigment can highlight the eyes and the main part that shows immediately around the eye is called the 'halo'. Occasionally this can be slow to darken in a young puppy, and even an adult can seem to lose this pigment at times. During a long winter with little sun, at times of illness or during a bitch's season, the black points such as the nose and eyerims can become quite pale. This is a major problem if you are intending to show or breed from your Bichon, but is of little importance to a family pet.

Pigment throughout the body has caused problems because some owners have become alarmed at big, dark patches appearing on their puppy's skin, which can be seen

Watch out for the mischievous twinkle in the eye which is so typical of the Bichon.

through the coat, especially when it is wet. People have been concerned that the dog has been injured and they are witnessing extensive bruising – and they are very relived to learn that this is perfectly normal.

TAILS WIN

The Bichon tail, quite besides being the most beautiful tail that can be seen on any dog, is often an indicator of your dog's mood. To look at, it is the plushest plume of long, thick hair that hangs over the back. It is supposed to lie along the back, almost like a huge ostrich feather. It barely touches the body but drapes over the the coat with the really long hair seen on the mature coat, falling loosely over the side. When the dog is moving it should stay held over the back and should never drop down behind. A drooping tail tells us just one thing: the Bichon is unhappy.

ON THE MOVE

There is a general understanding that a well-built Bichon, with the right conformation and with good muscle tone, will generally move correctly. Bichon movement is free flowing with the back legs moving parallel and the front legs reaching out in a straight and tidy manner. The elbows should not stick out or swing around as he

If a Bichon is built correctly, he will move correctly.

moves neither should his hocks turn in or out.

Whether your pet Bichon moves correctly or not will be of little concern to you as long as he moves at a comfortable speed and he is not lame for any reason. If your dog is destined for the show ring, or you are thinking about breeding, his movement and his ability to move correctly will be a major consideration.

Head carriage should be proud with the head held high, and with everything in balance. A Bichon should have a bit of

attitude and a spring in his step and look as if he is enjoying life to the full.

ASSESSING YOUR BICHON

To establish whether your dog is of sufficient quality to show, try attending a small informal companion dog show, or going to a breed club show or event. You should also find a local ringcraft class, which is an invaluable training ground for the novice exhibitor. Your vet will usually have contact details. These classes are not exclusive to show dogs either; anyone can go along and learn more about their breed. They are excellent places to socialise and train your puppy. You will learn the basics about holding the lead and teaching your dog to sit, as well as learning the particular way to show your dog that is suitable for your breed.

Bichons are table dogs, which means the judge will go over your dog on a table that is set at a comfortable height for examination. The judge will need to examine your dog closely all over to check that he has all the correct breed points. To allow this, your dog will need to stand quite still and allow a stranger to take a close look.

You will then need to move your dog smartly across the room, usually in a triangle, for the judge to assess his movement and character. There is a lot to learn but it can be great fun and a very good opportunity to meet new friends and like-minded people.

TEMPERAMENT

The typical Bichon temperament can be described as happy go lucky. He should never be nervous or unfriendly and should always be lively. His general demeanour should be of a very pretty dog greeting you with his tail wagging, looking very pleased and eager to meet you. A Bichon should never appear aloof or distant, and there should be no hint of aggression.

Bichons can be quite excitable and active which for some can be a little overwhelming, especially if they are barking excitedly or jumping up. The excitable side of a Bichon's temperament can be a disadvantage if you have very small children or you lead a particularly quiet or inactive life.

Another Bichon trait is a certain amount of possessiveness, which can make a poorly trained Bichon quite demanding. A dog can only be as well behaved as his owner's training allows, and a poorly trained Bichon can be noisy and attention-seeking if his behaviour is not curbed.

Like most Toy dogs, the Bichon likes the sound of his voice, but barking is usually reserved for letting you know that someone is at the door or that dinner is a little later than usual. A Bichon can be quite protective of his beloved family, and will make a

This is an active, high-spirited breed.

sterling little guard dog, ready to warn you of footsteps heard outside, or someone at the door.

The Bichon has a bigger bark than his size might suggest, and visitors are often surprised when they are greeted by a little dog after hearing a loud, deep bark. I find this invaluable when it comes to guarding the home, which nowadays has to be quite an important consideration.

A Bichon's temperament will also depend upon what he inherits from his parents. It is therefore vitally important to go to a reputable breeder that is known for producing dogs that are sound in both mind and body. *For detailed information on choosing a puppy, see Chapter Three.*

PEOPLE DOGS

A Bichon's chief desire is to be with you all the time, on your lap in the evening and at your side during the day, as your constant companion. Most Bichons are happy, lively and devoted little dogs that crave attention. They thrive on company and so breeders usually prefer to place a puppy in a family where at least one family member is at home during the day.

I would never recommend leaving a Bichon at home, alone all day, while you are out at work. He will almost certainly become distressed and unhappy. This kind of distress may manifest itself in several ways. Your Bichon may bark and howl, and you may be unaware of this until your irate

The Bichon is very much a 'people dog' and hates being left on his own.

neighbours inform you. Destructive behaviour is also common in this situation, as it is with most breeds of dog, and a bored and distressed dog will wilfully damage his surroundings through anxiety.

A far more breed specific manifestation of a distressed Bichon is urinating and defecating indoors. I am sure there is an explanation for this, but sometimes it can feel that the Bichon is punishing the owner in the most effective way he can for daring to go out without him. This problem is one of the hardest to overcome as, unlike

the basic toilet training that your puppy went through when he first arrived in your home, you are not present to scold when the offence is committed. Some Bichons chew their feet, which can be attributed to distress, although there are a number of medical reasons for this habit, too.

Some Bichons can cope with short periods alone, especially if they have another dog as a companion. However, look out for the telltale sign of your Bichon dropping his tail from its usual position over his back, to hanging loosely down between

his back legs, and you will know that your dog is uncomfortable about the prospect of being left on his own.

For information on training and behavioural problems, see Chapter Six.

LIVING WITH CHILDREN

I am always delighted to learn that a family with children is considering a Bichon. The Bichon is exceptionally good with children and can be very tolerant when playing with them. Their size makes them ideal playmates yet their stature and build is robust enough to cope.

However, I would say that a puppy is unsuitable for pre-school aged children. It is rare that children in this age group fully understand the limitations of a puppy and they can be too rough with them. The pre school age group also have very little true understanding that grabbing a puppy by his leg or pulling him around can cause much distress to a young puppy. A Bichon puppy is very small and therefore easy to pick up by the smallest child – but a wriggly puppy is very easy to drop, resulting in severe injury.

Families with very demanding, young children can rarely give a young puppy all the attention he needs to complete toilet training, and grooming and training often falls below acceptable levels.

After the age of around five, children generally develop a better understanding of how any animal can feel pain and discomfort if it not handled

FAMILY LIFE

Generally, a Bichon is better suited to living with older children.

Most Bichons will learn to live in harmony with the family cat.

correctly and treated with care and respect. Introducing a puppy into your family at just the right time can be most rewarding; it may also become a valuable part of your child's education with an opportunity to learn about the pleasures and responsibilities involved in dog ownership.

LIVING WITH OTHER ANIMALS

Bichons generally get on very well with other pets depending on the nature of what other pets you may have. If you have another breed of dog already, it is important to find out if they are likely to be compatible. There are some dogs, such as some of the larger breeds, that will not

tolerate little, lively Toy dogs so it is always wise to make sure.

I am often asked if Bichons get on well with other household pets, especially cats. Cats and Bichons seem to learn to get along quite well. However, an older cat that is well established in a household may not take too kindly to the introduction of a young puppy. You will need to make arrangements so that your older cat can escape to another room when things become lively.

My biggest concern about a household that has cats is the control of fleas. Bichons cannot tolerate any level of flea infestation and cats are prone to regular re-infestation, even when there are excellent flea control measures in place.

EXERCISE

Like any dog a Bichon requires a sensible amount of exercise and activity. However, his willingness to please means he will be content to accompany you on a long, energetic walk and yet be equally happy with a quiet stroll through the park. It is important to bear in mind that if your dog is to be fit and healthy, he must have adequate exercise. If you do not have a large garden where he can run and play, regular walks are essential if he is to remain well muscled and trim.

BICHONS IN THE COMMUNITY

Bichons can make excellent therapy dogs, working with patients in hospital or long term

The Bichon's handy size combined with his sweet temper makes him an ideal therapy dog.

residents in care homes. The Bichon's friendly nature and eagerness to please make him an ideal candidate, and I know many dogs that have excelled in this situation. The emotional and physical benefits of having regular contact with a dog, whether you actually live with the dog or whether you are just being visited regularly by a therapy dog, are now well documented. Many people, particularly the elderly and those who live alone of all ages rely heavily on the companionship and support they receive from owning a dog as delightful company as a Bichon Frisé.

HEARING DOGS

Because of their size, Bichons are often adopted and trained as hearing dogs for the Deaf. A hearing dog can effectively change the life of someone who is deaf in much the same way as dogs are used as guide dogs for the blind.

The dog is trained to respond to everyday sounds such as the telephone or the doorbell and alert his owner by drawing his attention to the source of the sound sometimes by touching their arm with his paw. The dog will also be trained to recognise danger sounds such as a fire alarm, burglar or even a carbon monoxide alarm. However, he will quite remarkably, indicate this in a very different way, giving a special danger alert signal which will be instantly recognised by his owner, who can then react and ensure his safety.

PERFECT COMPANION

The Bichon is an intelligent dog and shows great loyalty towards his owners. This is epitomised in the story of MJ, who saved the lives of her owners Ernie and Angela Gritto and their four children by alerting them to a fire that had started downstairs. This little dog had to conquer her own instincts for survival in order to protect her beloved owner, which only serves to illustrate how devoted and clever these little dogs can be.

Max started his training when he was just under 12 months of age and now he works as a fully fledged Hearing Dog.

THE FIRST BICHON FRISÉ

Chapter 2

Life for our dogs has not always been as easy as this captivating breed deserves. You could say that this is because of their extreme love of life and tenacity of spirit. It is a story of triumph over adversity.

The family of the Bichon consists of the Maltese, Bolognese, Havanese, Cotton Du Tulear, Lowchen (Little Lion Dog), and the Bichon Frisé. These are generally accepted to have descended from the Barbet or water spaniel.

The origin of the Bichon Frisé is thought to be ancient, as allusions to a small white dog, can be found in writings dating back more than two centuries BC.

It has been agreed that the Bichon was not indigenous to Spain, but was, in fact, to be found in the Mediterranean region. It was during the 15th century that sailors took the dogs to the islands of the Atlantic ocean, namely the Canary islands, and the Spanish mainland, using them as commodities for sale and barter.

Once there, they quickly became an established part of island life, and they became known to the populace as the 'Tenerife Teria'. Why this was changed is not clear, but it is thought that the name 'Bicho Tenerife' was adopted to give the dogs more standing with the dignitaries of the time. 'Bicho' literally translated means 'small animal', and this word was probably corrupted over time to 'Bichon'. The word 'Tenerife' was included after the largest island so we get the name 'Bichon Tenerife', which was retained through several centuries.

ROYAL FAVOURITES

The Bichon Tenerife, as it was now known, appeared in Italy again during the Renaissance, probably traded by sailors visiting ports of call. Once in Italy they soon became firm favourites of the noblemen and their ladies, as well as those who liked to emulate others of a higher position.

During the latter part of the 15th century and throughout the 16th century when France invaded Italy, the Bichon Tenerife was among the spoils of war taken home by the invaders.

The dogs were already popular with French ladies and gentlemen, and were also received with warmth and affection at the court of Francis I (1515-1547). However, it was Henry III (1574-1589) who reached the heights of idiosyncrasy by becoming so besotted with these small, white dogs that he could not bear to be parted from them for any length of time. So it became a familiar

The Duchess of Alba, Goya 1795.

the Spanish painter Bartolome E Murillo depicted a small, white dog in a painting called The Holy Family and The Little Bird. There are certainly many more instances, where small, white dogs are depicted in paintings, many of which have been reproduced on postcards. Whether these are indeed our Bichon, is left for the individual to decide.

When Napoleon III (1808-1873) came to the throne in 1851, the Bichon was as popular in royal circles as he had been during the reign of Henry III, almost three centuries before.

FALL FROM GRACE

The popularity and royal favour enjoyed by the Bichon continued until the latter part of the 19th century. Why they fell from grace is not clear. What is evident is that they were no longer a valued pet or a status symbol, and were no longer bathed, perfumed or pampered. So a new era for our Bichon began. The Bichon now became a street urchin – a common dog for the common people – and their once pure bloodlines became diluted. However, our dog is a born survivor and with his zest for life, coupled with his ability to learn, he quickly came to the attention of those who travelled with the circus and attended village fairs. Mrs Madelene Harper, writing for Our Dogs in 1982, says that on a visit to Russia three years earlier, she saw Bichons performing in a troupe at the Moscow State Circus. She goes on to say "their

sight at court to see the monarch conducting the business of the day with these little dogs recumbent in a basket which was tied around his neck with bright ribbons. The ladies of the court, wishing to curry favour with the monarch, took to keeping the little dogs about their person, either tucking them under an arm, or wrapping them into the fold of their gowns. These dogs were truly pampered pets of the time, being given every attention as to their comfort and welfare. Meanwhile the Bichon had found equal favour within the Spanish court. This is reflected in the

paintings of the time, most notably those by Francis Jose Goya (1746-1828). The Spanish artist became court painter to Charles IV in 1799, an appointment he retained until after the occupation of Spain by Joseph Bonaparte in 1814. Goya's painting of the Duchess of Alba is shown with a small, white dog standing by the embroidered hem of her floor length gown. A painting by Jean-Honore Fragamonde entitled The Love Letter, shows what is thought to be a Bichon, seated next to his mistress as she leans over a writing table. In the 17th century,

CHANGE OF FORTUNE

At the end of the First World War (1914-1918) French soldiers returning home from the battle fronts of Europe, brought with them the street dogs they had found so appealing. So once again fortune was to change for the Bichon, and he regained his role as a cherished and much loved pet. He very soon caught the eye of dedicated French and Belgian dog fanciers, who could see the potential these dogs afforded. So they began a carefully documented breeding programme using the best of the stock available to them.

In March 1933 a Breed Standard was drawn up by the president of the Toy Club of France, in conjunction with the Friends of the Belgian Breeds. This was accepted as the official Standard for the breed. At the same time it was now felt that 'Bichon Tenerife' was no longer an appropriate name and it should be changed. It was the president of the international Canine Federation who suggested 'Bichon a Poil Frisé'. Translated this means 'Bichon of the curly coat' which gave a much more descriptive view of the breed's characteristics, no longer identifying the dog as of Spanish origin.

Towards the latter end of 1934, the Bichon a Poil Frisé was admitted to the French Kennel Club Stud Book and listed by the Federation Cynologique International as a French/Belgian breed, having the right to be registered in the book of origins from both countries.

There is very little information as to the fate of the Bichon during the Second World War, but it is believed that breeding came to a virtual standstill. However, the Milton kennel owned by M and Mme Bellotte of Brussels had dogs documented from 1929 until 1976. Most of today's pedigrees can be traced back to this early breeding.

performance was outstanding and the little dogs had a wonderful time".

ARRIVAL IN THE UK

The breed began in the UK in 1974 when Mrs Elish Banks of the Cluneen prefix, an experienced and successful breeder exhibitor of Lowchens (a breed she helped establish), imported a bitch called Lejerdell Tarz Anna, born on June 3rd 1973. She was sired by Mex & Int Ch. Tarzand de la Persalere Dam Tenriffe de a Persalere, and bred in America by J & D Podell. This was the first Bichon Frisé to be exhibited both in England and Ireland. At her first show, one week out of quarantine, she won Best Not Separately Classified at the Leeds Championship Show, and in 1975 she became the first Bichon to be entered at Crufts. Mrs Banks went on to import several more Bichons; two from the Lejerdell kennel, one bitch and one dog, and then four bitches and one dog from the De Wanarbry kennel in France.

Meanwhile in 1973 Mr & Mrs Sorstien left America and took up residence in the UK. They brought with them their two dogs Rava's Regal Valor Of Reenroy and Jenny-Vive de Carlise. The following year on 3 March 1974, they produced a litter of five. These were the first British-born Bichon Frisé. From this first litter, Mrs Jackie Ransom of the the well-known Tresilva prefix and herself a breeder exhibitor of Poodles, chose two puppies, a dog Carlise Cicero and a bitch Carlise Circe. The dog Cicero won very well from the moment he entered the ring. At the Hammersmith Open Show on 6 October 1974 under judge Mr W.R. Irving, he won all his classes to go Best Puppy, and Reserve Best in Show. Mr Irving's critique was as follows: *"I very much admired this youngster which moved so well and with such smoothness and drive, good broad slightly rounded skull, correct body proportions, with the typical overbuilt tendency, which is required in the breed. I was well aware that there would be those who would ask afterwards what I knew about this breed which is so rare in the UK. But having seen quite a large number of them in the United States I felt confident that this was a good specimen and fitted well into the Breed Standard."*

Cicero was also the first Bichon to be pictured on the Vetzyme adverts.

Ch. Carlisle Cicero of Tresilva, owned by Jackie Ransom, and first exhibited in the UK in 1974.

From a repeat mating, three bitches and two dogs were born, on 1 March 1975. The three bitches all went as foundation stock to well respected breeders. Carlise Columbine went to the Glenfolly kennels of Mr & Mrs C Coley; Carlise Canny Caprise to Mrs E Myrlies of the Beaupres Pekingese, and Carlise Calypso Orion to Mrs Vera Goold who was already established in Fox Terriers with the prefix Sidewater. Mrs Goold joined forces with Mr Derick Chiverton under the new prefix Leijazulip, and two more dogs were imported later that year, Jazz de la Buthiere and Leilah de la Buthiere.

Mrs Ransom also imported a dog and bitch from Belgium, Zethus de Chaponay and Zena de Chaponay bred by Mr and Mrs Vansteenkiste-Delu. Zethus will be found in many of the pedigrees of today. He was also top stud dog in 1979. He died at the age of sixteen and a half, having led an extremely healthy life with never a visit to the vet.

Mrs Wendy Streatfield, owner of the Leander quarantine kennels, a very successful breeder of Poodles, and an expert groomer, had been involved with the breed since the early 1970s. In 1975 she brought in from the USA Am. Ch. C & D's Sunflower, bred by D. Wolske. While in quarantine she whelped a litter of four on the 9 September 1975, sired by Am. Ch. C & D's Beau Monde the Blizzard. In 1976 three more bitches were imported from America and in 1977 two more came from the Continent and two more from America. One of the latter, Am. Ch. Vogelflights Choirboy, born on 19 February 1975, was exhibited at the first ever Open Show held by the newly formed Bichon Frisé Club Of Great Britain. He won Best In Show under the celebrated judge Miss Graham-Weall MBE, and the critique read:

Jazz de la Buthiere: Imported to the UK and later went to Australia where be became a Champion.

Zethus de Chaponay of Tresilva: Imported from Belgium by Jackie Ransom.

"*I was very thrilled with my eventual winner Am. Ch. Vogelflights Choirboy of Leander. Seems to me to have every thing the breed needs, lovely head and eye, body shape, front and shoulder, very nice size, excellent texture coat, of course beautifully presented*".

At the same show one of the bitches born in quarantine Leander Beau Monde Snow Carol, owned in partnership with Miss Sally Wheeler, won reserve Best Bitch. Miss L Graham-Weall MBE wrote:

"*Very good bitch, lovely head and dark eye, good front, nice neck and shoulder, very good coat texture, shade long cast and not so positive in hind movement*".
Choirboy was a great ambassador for the breed and he went on to win many top

honours, including a Group win and Reserve Best In Show at Bath Championship Show – the first Bichon Frisé to achieve these awards. In all, 14 dogs were imported by the Leander kennels, 12 from the USA and two from the continent.

On a visit to the United States in 1973 Mrs Pauline Block, already prominent in Pharaoh Hounds and long coated Chihuahuas, had been invited to judge the Pharaoh Hound Specialty Show on Long Island. During her stay she was taken to an all breed show, where she saw the Bichon Frisé for the first time, and said:

"*My eyes lit apon these wonderful white, fluffy creatures and I was smitten and set about finding out how I could bring one home*".

But it was not until 1975 that she was offered a proven brood bitch, Cottonmops Jolie Ivette, bred by D. P. Beatty of the Braymore kennel. Jolie Ivette came into quarantine in whelp to Am. Ch. Cali-Cols Octavious Caeser, a son of Mex. Ch. Dapper Dan and Lyne Of Milton. On 19 November 1975 she whelped a litter of six while still in quarantine. Of these two went to established kennels, and two Mrs Block retained.

In 1977 a further two dogs were imported to the Twinley kennel – Aster De Chaponay and Amber De Chaponay. Astor was Reserve Best Dog at the first club show and Miss L. Graham-Weall MBE wrote:

"*Very good dog, lovely dark eye, good front, short back, deep brisket, good texture coat. A little more hair on his ears would complete the picture".*

In 1976 Mrs Madaline Harper of the Huntglen prefix (the top kennel in whole coloured King Charles) imported Zara De Chaponay, and Mrs Freda McGregor of Littlecourt (top kennel in Lowchens) imported Astrid De Chaponay and Astor De Villa Sainval. Astor's first show out of quarantine was memorable, winning Best Puppy In Show. Mr & Mrs K & B Rawlings chose their stock from Mme Laisne's kennel in France, where 1978 saw the arrival of Noe de Closmoynes and Nolie de Closmoynes. These were descendants of two dogs imported into Belgium from Tenerife in the 1940s. They also imported Int. Ch. If de la Buthiere, from Madame Desfarges.

In all a total of 40 dogs were imported, forming the foundation of the breed in the UK.

THE FIRST CHAMPIONS

IN 1980 the Kennel Club granted the breed six sets of Challenge Certificates, just six years from the introduction of the Bichon Frisé into the country, which was a phenomenally short time for any breed. The six Championship shows chosen were: Crufts, UK Toy Dog, Birmingham National, the Scottish Kennel Club, the Welsh Kennel Club, and Driffield Championship Show.

Ch. Gosmore Tresilva Zorba: The first Bichon to win a CC at Crufts.

CRUFTS

The first show, Crufts, was at that time held at Earls Court in London, and was to be judged by the eminent all-rounder and founder member of the Bichon Frisé Club of Great Britain, Mr Lionel Hamilton Renwick. Mr Renwick awarded Challenge Certificates in a variety of breeds, however his greatest interest was in Miniature Pinschers, where his Berlinga kennel had made quite an impact.

From the dogs, he chose Gosmore Tresilva Zorba sired by Zethus de Chaponay of Tresilva out of Carlise Circe of Tresilva, owned by Jackie Ransom and handled on the day by Geoff Corish. Zorba also went on to Best of Breed, and was in the final line up in the Toy Group which was judged by Mrs Catherine Sutton.

From the bitches, the top honours went to Glenfolly Silver Lady of Sarabande, sired by Leander Beaumonde Snow Puff out of Carlise Columbine. She was shown by her owner, Mrs Ann Worth. Silver Lady had been a prolific winner from her first appearance and triumph at the first Club show, where she won Best Puppy, Best Bitch and reserve Best in Show, at just 10 months old.

The reserve Challenge Certificate went to the young dog, Cluneen Jolly Jason from Hunkidori, sired by Cluneen Lejerdell Silver Starshine out of Cluneen Lejerdell Tarz Anna. Jason had already proved his worth in the show ring by becoming the first Bichon to gain a Junior Warrant. The bitch reserve Challenge Certificate went to Gosmore Tresilva Crystal, again sired by Zethus out of Tresilva Aura.

UK TOY DOGS SOCIETY

The second set of Challenge Certificates were to be awarded by Terry Thorn, at the UK Toy Dogs Society. Terry Thorn's breed was Salukis, but he awarded Challenge Certificates to various breeds within the Hound, Working, Utility and Toy Groups.

Top honours went to the same four dogs, so this was to make the third more interesting than ever.

JUDGE'S CRITIQUE: BIRMINGHAM NATIONAL

The breed this time was to be judged by Andrew Brace, well known international judge, who had judged the breed the previous year at Bath Canine Society. This is what he had to say:

"I suppose I had a difficult job in having to award the third set of tickets, as those third tickets could make up two Champions. Really speaking no way could I win, as if I did the same dogs I would be accused of following fashion, and if I did something different I would be accused of trying to be sensational. As it was, I tried to judge the dogs as I saw them on the day. I had the biggest entry of Bichons ever seen in the UK to date with 73 dogs, making 113 entries.

"The quality was high right through, and it amazed me how the breed had managed to level off in just a year. Most of my winners were well-balanced with the right heads and good coats, though they had all been barbered far more than the Standard really allows.

"When it came to my dog Challenge, I was torn between two. Zorba had taken the open dog class, but in limit I had a youngster who was a complete stranger to me. I thought he was quite breathtaking – beautiful outline, superb movement and just no exaggeration anywhere – total quality and fabulous ring presence.

"Zorba's head is classic and that is really his outstanding point. He has a good coat texture but in the Challenge I felt his front action could not match the limit dog, Leijajulip Kipling of Shamaney, and he didn't have the youthful sparkle and zest. Thus it was that I decided on Kipling for the ticket and Zorba for the reserve. I felt for Jackie Ransom and sporting Geoff Corish, his handler, as they had obviously hoped to make Zorba into the first Champion in the UK, but I genuinely felt unable to do so on the day.

"In bitches, Gosmore Tresilva Crystal won limit and Silver Lady the open class. Crystal is exquisite for type and, like Zorba, she has a dreamy head and eyes. She is so typey all through but her hind action did really let her down. Silver Lady is now more finished than she was at Bath when I just gave her a first, and she has a pleasing head and is very sound on the move. She is a tough bitch to fault. On the day I felt she deserved the ticket, and consequently her Championship. History had been made, and I was happy to have played a part in it.

"For Best of Breed I still could not get past Kipling and he was kept in the final four in the Group under Bob Flavell, which pleased me no end. We now have our first Champion, and the breed is going from strength to strength. When I analysed my results I discovered that I had put up both Continental and American bred dogs so it is obvious that both can produce the same type which appeals".

Mrs Vera Goold bred Leijazulip Kipling of Shamaney who was sired by Leijazulip Guillaume out of Ninon de la Buthiere of Leijazulip, owned by Mrs Flintoft Black.

SCOTTISH KENNEL CLUB

The fourth set of tickets were awarded by the first breed specialist, Wendy Streatfield. She also owned the Kerry Blue Terrier, Ch. and Am. Ch. Calla Ghan of Leander, imported from the USA who went Best in Show at Crufts in 1979.

A new dog took the top spot in Montravia Persan Make Mine Mink, sired by If de la Buthiere of Antarctica out of Leander Pleasures Persan, bred by Mrs Bernice Perry, and owned by Mrs Pauline Gibbs. There was a fourth ticket for Silver Lady. On this occasion, Kipling had to be content with the reserve ticket.

For the bitches, it was Persan Pearl Button of Si'bon, sired by Am. Ch. Vogleflights Choirboy of Leander out of Leander Dora Persan. She was bred by Mrs Bernice Perry and owned by Mrs Marion Binder.

The following is Mrs Streatfield's critique:

"It was a great pleasure for me to be the first breed specialist to award CCs to the Bichon Frisé; I regretted the lack of opportunity to discuss with the exhibitors the reasons for my particular assessment and placings of their dogs. I must agree with Mr Brace's observation that the breed would benefit from a year or two's grace before accepting certificates and I found this judging assignment quite a tough one as a considerable diversity of type is still prevalent. Nevertheless, I noted an overall improvement since last year which is certainly encouraging.

"There is a tremendous variation in heads and eyes and although I accept that a long, snipey face deviates from the Standard, I personally find the ultra short heads with the inevitable lack of muzzle quite ugly, particularly if coupled with eyes set too far apart, or too large and bulging. I still cannot condone a light eye! Although I am aware that assessment of expression is influenced by individual preference, to me it is of paramount importance. In my opinion, if a Bichon has an appealing expression, length of muzzle or eye placement deviating slightly from the Standard, it will be, to me, of secondary importance.

"I have frequently commented on lack of ring presence and style in this breed, and therefore I was delighted to find several dogs showing the emergence of this important quality, and it was this very quality that I found in my CC and reserve CC winners in dogs. I was also gratified to see improvement in hindquarters; these have been a major fault so often in the past.

"I would think it wrong to discourage the presentation and scissoring of coats, providing that the correct coat length is adhered to, for the fact we are able to present the Bichon in such an immaculate condition has proved a contributing factor to their rapid gain in popularity. Careful presentation can transform what would be a fairly nondescript little dog into a classy, eye catching Bichon Frisé. I was delighted to find every exhibit happy and carefree in temperament. I am certain we would all agree that this equable temperament, so special to this breed, must be maintained and nurtured.

"In retrospect I feel it was a great pity the classification was not divided into separate dog and bitch classes, as it has been so hard this year for people to qualify for Crufts, and every opportunity was needed".

WELSH KENNEL CLUB

This time it was Mrs Muriel Lewin officiating, highly respected for her Elwin Maltese. Gosmore Tresilva Zorba gained his third ticket thus gaining his title of Champion – the first dog to do so. The bitch CC went to Montravia Snow Dream, sired by Ch. Montravia Snow Fox out of Montravia Leander Snow Princess. The reserve CCs went to Montravia Persan Make Mine Mink, and Beaupres Blithe Spirit of Bochin. The latter was bred by Mrs E & Miss Fiona Mirylees, sired by Zethus de Chaponay of Tresilva out of Carlise Canny Caprice of Beaupres.

DRIFFIELD

The final set of tickets for 1980 was down to Graham Newall, a committee member of the Bichon Frisé Club of Great Britain and owner of Twinley Jolie Posie, one of the bitch puppies born in quarantine. His Dohkam kennel of Tibetan Terriers was known worldwide.

The dog ticket went to Gosmore Tresilva Zorba and, once again, Silver Lady took the bitch ticket, giving her five of the six Challenge Certificates on offer for the year. Reserve CCs went to Clunean Jolly Jason and Montravia Snow Dream.

So for the first year, one dog and one bitch made it to their title.

In 1981 the breed received six sets of tickets, and two more Champions were made up. Cluneen Jolly Jason took three of the tickets, and Persan Make Mine Mink gained the two he needed to make him up. For the bitches, Montravia Snow Dream took five of the six Challenge Certificates on offer. The breed now had five Champions, three dogs and two bitches.

In 1982 there were 12 sets of Challenge Certificates on offer and these increased, year on year. In 1990, just 10 years after the

Ch. Glenfolly Silver Lady of Sarabande: The first Champion made up in the UK.

Kennel Club granted the breed Championship status, 27 sets of CCs were on offer. By the end of 2007, 177 dogs had gained their titles. By the end of 2008, 188 Bichons had gained their titles.

BICHONS IN THE US

The Bichon Frisé arrived in the USA in 1956, 23 years before the first dogs were imported into the UK. But unlike the UK, The road to full recognition by the American Kennel Club in 1973 was long, hard and frustrating, and we can only be grateful that those early breeders continued to champion their cause.

However once they were groomed and trimmed to present a more glamorous outline from the original rather dishevelled look, their rise in popularity, as in the UK, was spectacular.

The breed began in 1956 when

Mr & Mrs Pickult left their home in France to join their children in America. They took with them their three Bichons, two males and a female. One of the males, Eddie White de Steron Vor (Int. Ch. Bandit de Steron Vor – Ami du Larry) and the female Etoile de Steron Vor (Int. Ch de Steron Vor – Criquette de Steron Vor) were purchased from the kennels of Mme Abadie before they left France.

Once in America and settled, Eddie and Etoile were mated and she duly produced a litter of five puppies.

In 1958 one of the bitches called Hermine de Hoop went to Mrs Azalia Gasgoine. Then in 1962 Mrs Gasgoine visited the Paris dog show, and while there met Madamoiselle Milligari, with the result that she brought back three more bitches which included Lady of Frimoussette When mated to Andre de Gasgoine, another Eddie and Etoile son, she produced Dapper Dan de Gasgoine, one of the most dominant sires of the time, siring 17 Champions. Dapper Dan is behind many of the early dogs. Mrs Gertrude Fournier, a noted breeder of Collies under the Cali-Cols prefix, acquired four of the Pickults dogs, and in 1962 imported two sisters, Lassie and Lyne of Milton. Later to be

The breed was established in the USA before making its debut in the UK. These are the foundation dogs of the Chaminade line.

joined by a dog, Marquis of Milton. These two ladies were a great force in the breed. Mrs Gasgoine was the first president and Mrs Fournier the first secretary and registrar of the newly formed Bichon Frisé Club of America. When Mrs Fournier was 80 she came to the UK to judge Best Puppy and Best In Show at the Special Open Show held as a prelude to the first international congress on the breed.

RECORD HOLDERS
There have been many notable records achieved by breeders and exhibitors in all breeds and all countries and the Bichon is no exception to this. Am. Ch. Chaminade Mr Beau Monde is one of these. Bred by Barbara Stubbs, and owned by Mr Richard Beauchamp and Pauline Waterman, he lived to the age of 14 and sired an amazing 65 champions. These in turn produced 205 Champions. The descendants of these dogs had a great influence on the breed, being the foundation stock of kennels both in America and the UK. In the mid-80s, Am. Ch. Devon Puff and Stuff, owned and bred by Nancy Shapland, was to break all records in the show ring, notching up 60 Best in Show's, 165 Groups and winning the Bichon Frisé Club of America National Specialty. She was Top Bichon in 1985 and again in 1986, and also that year Top Non Sporting. Her record will surely

never be beaten.

Strictly speaking the next two dogs were not born and bred in America, but do deserve a mention. The first was bred in the UK by Mrs Wendy Streatfield in 1976, and went to Mr & Mrs Mackenzie Begg in Australia. In 1979, Mr Richard Beauchamp was on a judging tour of five different countries, among them Australia. Here is an extract from an article written about his tour.

"In Australia I judged Bichon Frisé, I had a record entry for that country of 28. Considering quarantine regulations and that the breed has only been in Australia a total of two years I consider it a remarkable entry. The dog I found in the junior class and eventually carried to

Am Ch. Devon Puff and Stuff: Top winning Bichon in the US with a remarkable tally of 60 Best in Show wins.

Eng. Ir. Ch. Tiopepi Mad Louie at Pamplona: A recent Breed record holder with 26 CCs.

Best of Breed was the finest specimen of the breed that I had seen anywhere in the world. He was the result of American bloodlines, though bred in England and exported to Australia as a pet. His name is "Aus Ch Leander Snow Star".

At six years of age, he went to Laura Purnell (Tomaura Bichons) in America, where he was once again a prolific winner and one of the top sires, with 33 champions to his credit. The other is Ch Si'bon Sloan Ranger at Pamplona, bred by Mrs Marion Binder and owned by Mr Michael Coad. In 1988 he gained his title in Britain, winning five CCs and three Reserves. He then went out to Jill and Stan Cohen where he

gained his American title in three days. He is believed to be the first Bichon to become a Champion in both countries.

THE BREED TODAY

The Bichon Frisé has been in the UK now for just over 35 years, so we are still in real terms a young breed.

When the breeders first imported the dogs there were preferences of type which was only natural. This also extended to the show ring and to presentation. Those who had imported from America favoured their style of grooming, and certainly those breeders and exhibitors of Poodles preferred the more glamorous end result that showed off the dogs' outline. There is no doubt this

style of presentation made Bichons stand out in the ring and gave them many admirers outside the show scene.

On the other hand, there were those who resisted this and preferred to abide by the standard of the country of origin and only 'tidy up'. However it soon became apparent that the majority of new exhibitors and judges preferred the more stylish presentation, and so gradually all conformed. Presentation today is a far cry from those early days, some would say we have now gone too far and the dog has become 'stylised' with no thought for the breed standard.

The dogs in the beginning were a very mixed bag, long and low with beautiful heads and pigment

THE BREED TODAY

Ch. Bobander What A Performance, winner of 15 CCs and 7 Best of Breeds, bred and owned by Chris Wyatt (Bobander Bichons).

UK & US Ch. Manoir's Shot in the Dark, JW (Bullet), winner of Multiple Best of Breed in both the UK and the US. Group 1 LKA Championship Show 2009 (UK), Group 1 placements in USA. CAC Winner at World Show 2008. Bullet is owned and handled by Pauline Johns, Manoir Bichons.

Norwegian Ch.& Swedish Ch. Peti Ami's Devils Rose ('Festus'), owned and bred by Wivi Anne Olson in Norway. He was Norway's 'Dog of the Year' in 2008.

Photo: Steinar T Moen.

but not so positive in hind movement, larger dogs with plainer heads, and lighter eyes, pigment not so intense, but lovely movement. Coat texture was also very mixed and ranged from the very soft and curly to the extremely harsh, that stayed exactly as it was scissored.

However the early pioneers were all experienced breeders, and slowly the breed came together, and by the early 90s the breed was more uniform in size and more of a type, with less and less of the short-legged long-backed dogs in evidence. There were some truly beautiful dogs that could take their place in any company. Our dogs were also sought after in other parts of the world, and along with young stock some of our top winners and proven studs were exported.

Today, with the demise of quarantine and the introduction of the pet passport allowing freedom of travel, the breed is again being influenced by dogs from abroad. Whether this will be good for the breed only time will tell.

There is one thing that has not changed and that is the Bichons themselves. They have never lost their good temperament, charm, personality and loyalty, and that is why they will continue to attract followers from all walks of life.

CURRENT REGISTRATIONS
The breed has had a high profile image from the introduction of the first dogs into the UK, from

From small beginnings, the Bichon Frisé is now among the most popular of Toy dogs. *Photo: Steve Jefford (The K9 Breed Bar Photography).*

those breeders who saw the potential of the breed and expended a great amount of time to import them, to the BFC of Great Britain, whose list of founder members reads very much like the 'who's who' of the dog world.

But could anyone have foreseen just how quickly they would rise in popularity? Or how all who saw them would take them to their hearts, both for exhibition and as companions? Kennel Club registrations show a huge rise in popularity since the first Bichon Frisé (Espour du

Klosiers, owned by Mr & Mrs Hobart) was registered in 1957. Between 1974 (following the importation of the breed) and 1976 there were only 31 registrations, but over the next twenty years, the breed's popularity grew until, by 1996, registrations had reached 2,758.

The number of registrations varies slightly each year, as does its position in the list of most popular breeds, but the Bichon remains consistently in the 'most popular' list and registrations seem to be following an upward annual trend.

A BICHON FOR YOUR LIFESTYLE

3 Chapter

A Bichon is a lively, happy, little extrovert who is almost certainly going to change your life completely. Bichons want to love you and please you and, as such, can often be very demanding until they realise just what it is you want from them. It is essential therefore, that you consider just how much time and attention your new dog will need, and how these demands will fit around your existing lifestyle, before you take the big step of acquiring a bundle of energy that will have you in fits of laughter one minute and drive you round the bend the next!

GIVING TIME
Caring for a Bichon can be very time consuming, so consider carefully whether you can commit to caring for your pet for the next 15 or so years. If your family is still very young or you intend to add to your family, will you be able to maintain the same standard of care and attention if there is a new baby in the family?

The structure of a family will change naturally and, although you may be at home with a young family now and see a family pet as a lovely addition, what of the future? Are you likely to return to a demanding career when the children are a little older? Or is a move abroad likely? All these twists and turns in life can happen and we deal with them as they occur, but Bichons, in particular, do not like being left on their own while everyone is at work or at school. If this is your plan, the Bichon Frisé is not the dog for you.

If your intention is to purchase a Bichon as a companion, as so many people do, because the family has grown up and left home, then a Bichon is perfect for you. Their needs and demands fit well into the general lifestyle of those who are soon to reach retirement age, and many people decide to wait until they are at home during the day before they commit to dog ownership.

If you live alone, perhaps a little consideration should be given to how your Bichon could be cared for should you go into hospital. If you do not have a willing family member or a friend who can help out, there are many pet sitters who can take care of your pet in either their own home or in yours when required. There are dog walkers and kennels that specialise in Toy dogs that can be called upon should your absence from home be necessary. However, you should allow your Bichon to get to know his 'carer' before you actually need one. Living alone should not prohibit you from enjoying the companionship of a

Bichon. If you are just taking a holiday, there are many hotels in the UK that welcome dogs, especially Bichons who can win over most people with their charm.

A SUITABLE HOME
Is your home 'pet friendly'? Unfortunately we are not all lucky enough to live down a quiet leafy lane, with no neighbours, in an acre of walled garden. Whether you live in the city or the country, Bichons, because of their smaller size and adaptability, can cope well with most different types of surroundings. Flats can be a problem, however, because all dogs need access to an area where they can relieve themselves and to deny this to any dog can lead to all sorts of problems. Bichons are Toy companion dogs; they are not suited to being kennelled or to being kept outside alone for long periods. They need to be indoors, with you.

Exercising your bichon is essential as, like children, they need to use up their energy. Bichons will walk for as long as you want them to, but this is not good for them. When young, dogs should only be walked for short periods of time, no more than 30 minutes. Over

The Bichon is an adaptable little dog and will suit most types of home.

walking them can cause developmental problems for their bones and can lead to difficulties in old age. As your pet gets older you can extend the walk but this should never be for more than one hour at a time. As a rule it is better to do a few short walks than one long one. You should also be prepared to find time at intervals during the day to play with your puppy so that he doesn't get bored. This can help stop him becoming destructive and chewing things. If he starts chewing your favourite shoes, firmly remove the shoe, and replace with something he is allowed to chew – a toy shoe of his own or a bone to cut his teeth on.

Some breeders are very reluctant to sell puppies (and sometimes even older dogs) to families with young children. Unless children have been brought up in an environment where they have had contact with animals, they may not have the necessary discipline or understanding of how to deal with a living breathing animal and may just regard it as another toy. Bichons are very lively, energetic puppies that can sometimes over power young children and can even be accused of 'biting' when they are just playfully testing their new teeth. When viewing puppies the breeder will be able to assess whether the children will be able to cope with this new responsibility and whether the family is in fact suitable for the puppy. As a rule the majority of breeders prefer to find homes for their puppies with children over five years of age.

COUNTING THE COST
When deciding if a Bichon is the breed for you, it is important to take cost into consideration. Besides the initial outlay of purchasing your puppy, there will be additional costs involved which you need to budget for.

VETERINARY FEES

When you take on a dog, you must be able to pay for routine preventative health care, which includes vaccinations, worming and flea treatment. We are fortunate that the Bichon is one of the most healthy breeds, but being a living, breathing creature, your dog could become ill or have an accident. It is your responsibility as his owner and carer to seek medical help should your pet need it. Pet insurance is readily available and I strongly advise you to look into this as veterinary fees can be expensive. If you are not happy with any of the insurances available a good alternative is to place a set amount every month into a special bank account. Hopefully, you willÅpurchase a fit puppy that will grow into a healthy adult and, thankfully, most of the time this is indeed the case. However, it is important to guard against future contingencies.

Work out the financial implications involved in owning a Bichon before you make a firm decision.

FEEDING

The Bichon is only a small dog, so the cost of food is not a major consideration, but you must be able to provide a good-quality diet that is suited to your Bichon's needs. Bichons are very fond of vegetables and these can be given as treats or as a supplement to their regular dog food. *See Chapter Five: The Best of Care.*

GROOMING

Your pet will need grooming on a regular basis and this should be started as soon as you get your puppy home. You will need a slicker brush, pin brush and metal comb which are readily available in a variety of shapes and sizes from your local pet store. Costs vary considerably but as a rule each item should not be more than £10. The slicker brush and comb are needed to get through a dirty or knotted coat, whereas a pin brush is used just to brush the coat gently once all knots have been removed. You should try to make time every day to get your puppy used to being groomed so that no knots get out of hand. If done regularly this does not have to take very long. A lot of groomers lay the dogs down to groom them but this is something you should experiment with to find which position is most comfortable for you and your pet. You must be able to get under his legs and behind his ears as these are the areas that will be most likely to matt. A quality grooming spray can be helpful and stops the coat from breaking. If you find it difficult to cope with the grooming and trimming then there are many groomers who will take on the task for you, at a cost, but all bichons should be trimmed every six to eight weeks.

HOLIDAYS

If you are going away on holiday, you may be able to take your Bichon with you. There are now many hotels and cottages to rent which welcome pets. However, if you cannot take your Bichon on holiday, you will have to make other arrangements. Bichons are

There is not a significant difference in temperament between the male and female Bichon.

not particularly suited to general kennels as their coat needs constant attention and the majority of kennels do not know how to cope with a Bichon coat when it's dry let alone if it gets wet!

You may find that there is a small-dogs kennel or even someone locally, who will either live in your house to look after your pet or have your Bichon in their home. Again, this is something that should be

thought about and investigated before taking on a pet. Some Bichon breeders will even board their own puppies. Having your Bichon properly looked after when you are away, can be very costly but there are many options available. Your vet or breeder should be able to advise you on the best options in your area.

Bear in mind, it is not advisable to think about having a puppy if you are also planning a holiday. It is very important that a puppy

has time to adjust and settle in his new home before you vanish for a couple of weeks on holiday.

MALE OR FEMALE?
Before choosing your pet, you should consider whether you prefer a male or female to live with you. Although in some breeds there is a distinct difference in temperament, this is not the case with the Bichon Frisé. Both sexes are very affectionate and loving and

MORE THAN ONE?

Many people choose to have more than one Bichon. They are such wonderful companions that we find people come back time and time again and often end up with two or three to keep them company. Some people like to do it all in one go and have two from one litter, either two brothers together or two sisters together. I do not advise you to have one dog one bitch as this can lead to very difficult times. Trying to keep them apart when the bitch puppy is first in season, as most vets do not spay bitches until they have had at least one season, can be very trying. If you are not careful you could end up with puppies and this would not be healthy for the bitch or the puppies. If you decide you would like to add another Bichon to your family it is always better to bring in a youngster rather than an older dog as it is easier to introduce a puppy into the hierarchy in the family, whereas an older dog will try to assert himself above those already in the home and this does not always go down well with the resident Bichon. It is not just the males that argue over who is top dog – the bitches can be just as determined not to be usurped by a newcomer, so at whatever age you introduce another dog to the family it must be done sensibly and carefully. A lot of fuss and attention should be given to all, not just the new addition. Usually after a couple of days they will have sorted themselves out and everything will be fine as they are such amicable creatures and will enjoy having a companion to play with. Bichons remain playful most of their life but it is well to remember that as they get older they may not appreciate having a very young puppy pulling at them, so do not leave it too late to add a new member. If your pet is over 12 years of age perhaps wait until nature has taken its course. Some Bichons will be able to cope with a newcomer at any age, but you should give this some consideration when thinking of adding a new member to the family.

desperately want to please you. Bitches' temperaments can vary considerably when they have their seasons; some will be quieter and more precious about themselves, others will be like whirling dervishes and will be on the look out for a male friend. It won't matter to them whether he's a pedigree or not, so extra care must be taken when exercising bitches on heat. In fact over the crucial 10th day up to the 20th day it is sometimes best not to take them off your premises. The length of a season can vary. What is considered as normal – approximately three weeks from swelling – can drag on for four weeks, before they can happily mix with the opposite sex again. There is often a period of time when the bitch that hasn't been mated thinks she should have been and can suffer a phantom pregnancy. Her stomach swells as if there are puppies there and milk is even produced. This can be avoided if you have your bitch spayed. However this can often cause your bitch to put on a lot of weight. If you have a male dog that has not been neutered you will find he will become restless and often howl and whine if he gets the scent of a bitch in season anywhere in the local vicinity. However, as with humans, male dogs are prone to prostrate problems and this can be avoided by neutering your pet. Entire dogs will leave their scent and spray over where any bitches have passed. However, neutered dogs tend to put on weight and can easily become obese. This is one of the contributory factors to the increase of diabetes in dogs, so should you decide to have your pet neutered then you must be extremely careful with his diet.

Many prospective new owners will already have a definite idea about their personal choice of gender for their new puppy, but there is often very little substance other than "we have always had bitches in the past" or "we already have a boy's name for a new puppy". If it is your intention to take on a family companion, with no thoughts about breeding or showing, then my advice would be to keep an open mind because neutering your pet would be the sensible route to take in either case.

SHOW PUPPY

The vast majority of Bichons are bought and bred as pets, but there are some that are bred and kept for exhibition at dog shows, which are held all over the country. If this is the sport of your choice, then this will affect your choice of breed and where you will purchase your puppy. Bichons make terrific little show dogs because of their great character and attractive appearance, but showing is costly and competitive, so you need to find a puppy that has show potential.

If you are hoping to show your puppy you must stress this when talking to the breeder. It is impossible for any breeder to guarantee that a puppy will be suitable for showing. It is only possible to hope the puppy will grow into a stunning show dog if it has all the requirements of the breed standard. It is important therefore that you read and study the breed standard before you start looking for a show puppy. The basic requirements for a puppy are that it has a broad skull with large, dark, clear eyes, good pigmentation round its eyes, black nose and lips and black pads. The puppy should stand confidently and be forward looking, holding his tail over his back but never touching the back. One of the biggest problems is teeth, as a perfect scissor bite (upper teeth overlapping the bottom teeth) is required for showing and even though this can be perfect at eight weeks of age, occasionally when the adult teeth come through, around five months, this can go horribly wrong and suddenly you have a puppy you cannot show. The puppy's temperament is of the utmost importance as unless he is happy and outgoing there is no way he will be suitable for showing. Whether for showing or just as a much loved pet, your Bichon should in effect choose you by being the one most in your face and ready to play.

You should make sure you find a breeder/kennel that has a really good reputation for producing top-quality show dogs as it is very difficult to claim that a puppy at the tender age of eight weeks is going to be a quality

The breeder will help you to assess a puppy to see if he has show potential.

It is virtually impossible to predict how good a Bichon is going to be until he reaches full maturity.

show dog. Most respected breeders will only claim that the puppy possesses some 'show potential'.

BREEDING TERMS
If you choose to have a bitch puppy and you wish to breed from her, you must again make sure that your breeder is aware of this as most good breeders endorse their puppies, with the Kennel Club as 'progeny not to be registered'. The most responsible breeders do this in an attempt to stop their puppies ending up in the hands of

disreputable people who breed indiscriminately. This can result in some poor-quality, odd-looking Bichons with dubious temperaments, and many health problems.

FINDING A BREEDER
The Kennel Club keeps a record of all puppies registered with them and upon request will send you a list of all Bichon puppies available at the current time. The Kennel Club can also give you information regarding where shows are being held, where you can see the breed you are

interested in. This information is also available from *Dog World* and *Our Dogs* newspapers. When visiting a show you will be able to see different types and ascertain the type of dog that you prefer. If you then make a note of the name of these breeders you can approach them and discuss with them your preferences and they in turn can ascertain if they feel you would be suitable. However try not to talk to them until they have finished showing their dogs as there is a lot of preparation that goes into showing a Bichon and they need to concentrate,

Do your homework and wait until you find a breeder that has a reputation for producing sound, typical puppies.

It is important therefore to see the pedigree of the puppies and discuss this thoroughly with the breeder. If anyone tells you they have a litter of coloured Bichons, you should be alarmed! A pure bred Bichon is only ever white. Puppies often have peach patches on their ears and sometimes their body coat, but this will usually vanish by the time they are a year old.

Puppies are usually viewed at around four weeks, it is not normally advisable to visit before this as the puppies are very susceptible to infection when very young and they do not open their eyes until approximately two weeks of age. The puppies are usually weaned from their mothers at around five to six weeks so that by the age of eight weeks they are happily feeding themselves and ready to go to their new homes.

Puppies purchased from home breeders are usually easier to train and have been better socialised than those reared in kennels. The mere fact that they have been reared indoors, amongst people means they are more used to everyday events such as cleaning, TV and radio noise and the general bustle of a home, especially if there are children or grandchildren in the home. All this means they will find it easier to leave their littermates and settle in their new home. You must however, be prepared for several sleepless nights, as all puppies fret when they first leave their siblings and will find it very strange being on

but as a rule will be happy to discuss their progeny with you. They can then keep you informed of any litters they may be planning and if necessary place you on their waiting lists. Many of the top breeders have waiting lists because it is rare to have more than one or two puppies in a litter that are show quality and they may only have a couple of litters a year so their pups will always be in demand.

It may not always be possible to find one in your immediate vicinity and you may have to be prepared to travel to find the required puppy.

VIEWING THE LITTER
If when visiting the puppy for the first time you do not feel at ease then you should not feel pressurised into purchasing from

these premises. The number of puppies in a litter can vary considerably; the most puppies registered to one bitch are 12 but this is very rare. A normal sized litter is between three and seven puppies. You should be able to see all the litter, when the puppies are under eight weeks of age, and the mother of the puppies. The sire of the litter is not often on the premises as, very often, the breeder will have gone to a stud dog that lives some distance away. The aim is to find a male that is most likely to complement the bitch – not the one that lives closest to the breeder! Sometimes breeders keep two separate breeding lines within their kennels, and in these instances, a stud dog based at the kennel may be used.

It is important to see the mother with her puppies.

Spend time watching the puppies so you get an idea of their individual personalities.

their own in their new environment. Plenty of patience and understanding is required but you must be firm and get your puppy used to being where you have decided its new bed is to be (don't give in and take them to bed with you if you are not prepared for this to be a permanent fixture!!!) You must also get your new arrival used to being left on their own for short periods of time. It is best to do

this gradually leaving them a little longer each time you go out. Your Bichon has to fit into your life style not you into theirs! Regardless of whether the puppies have been reared in the home or in a kennel environment, the area they are kept in should be scrupulously clean and it should smell fresh. Watch out for the following signs of good health as you watch the puppies:

- Energetic and playful
- Clean, fluffy coat
- Confident on their feet
- Bright, clear eyes
- Solid stools

HEALTH CHECKS
We are very lucky with our Bichons, as there are very few health problems within the breed. We are not required by the Kennel Club to carry out any specific testing, although the

A responsible breeder will carry out health checks on all breeding stock.

majority of good breeders are now testing for Juvenile Cataracts, as there has been a slight increase in cases within the breed in the last few years. Bichons also suffer from tear staining. Vets often try to put this down to tear duct problems, and will recommend having the tear ducts operated on, but I have never heard of this being completely successful. The best way to treat the staining is to bathe the eyes on a regular basis and apply either Vaseline or tearstain removal cream (produced by the breed clubs) to the coat. This is only a way of preventing the staining of the

coat it will not stop the eyes watering. As I mentioned earlier we have noticed an increase in the amount of dogs in general which suffer from diabetes. This can be controlled, but it is far better to avoid the problem in the first place by being very careful with your dog's diet. The other problems occasionally encountered include patella luxation, Legge Perthes Disease and hip dysplasia. *For more information, see Chapter Eight: Happy and Healthy.*

AN OLDER DOG
There are many reasons why someone will suddenly decide

they cannot cope with their dog any longer. Sometimes it is ill health, financial problems, marriage break-up, or the need to return to work. The list is endless and the poor dogs do not understand what is happening to them. There are several rescue clubs which can help in these circumstances.

Taking on an older dog can be very rewarding for both of you, as you avoid the worry (in most cases) of having to house-train a puppy. It will be a learning time for you both, as the dog will have to get used to a new environment and routine, but this is all part of the fun of

It may suit your lifestyle to take on an older dog.

having a Bichon for company. Sometimes it can be difficult for older people to find a pet to keep them company, as they do not want the worry of a puppy but desperately want the company of a dog, so it is ideal for them to be able to take on an older Bichon.

Many breeders will part with their dogs as they get older, in order to give more attention to their new hopefuls, and because it is better for a dog to have his own home, where he will get individual attention, rather than being one of many. Most breeders only let a bitch have three or four litters and will then rehome her to avoid accidental matings in the future.

THE NEW ARRIVAL

Chapter 4

So you have done your homework on various breeds and decided on a Bichon. You will be collecting your new puppy shortly, or eagerly waiting to be selected for a rescued Bichon, so now is the time to make preparations for the new arrival. Some Bichons are very mischievous, others are calmer – and while some will never try to escape, there are others that have Houdini traits. For the purpose of preparing your home you should assume the worst!

GARDEN SAFETY

The first thing to check is garden fencing and gates, particularly those that lead to an unsecured area. Bichon puppies are capable of crawling under a tiny gap in a fence or under a gate. Adults may be 'jumpers' and can scale a three-foot (one-metre) gate with

ease. Some Bichons are diggers, and will easily tunnel their way under a fence where there is soft soil.

Take time to inspect all the boundaries in your back garden. Wooden fencing is ideal but sometimes the baseboard is level with the soil. Try digging a tunnel with a small garden spade; if you make the start of a tunnel into your neighbour's garden, a persistent Bichon will do the same with ease. A simple and cheap method of blocking this escape route is to purchase concrete paving slabs. Dig a 12-inch (30-cm) trough beside the fence, place the slabs vertically into the trough and fill in with soil, compressing it down well.

Wire fencing may present similar problems. Chain-link fencing is fine but never use chicken wire; it is not strong enough and if a puppy gets his paw stuck, it can cause a nasty

cut. The finer the wire, the sharper it is.

Check all gates that provide an exit route from your garden. If you have more than a 3-in (7-cm) gap under a gate you must fix it. Either lower the gate or fix a solid piece of wood to the bottom to fill in the gap. If your gate is only 3-ft (1-m) high you need to replace it with a taller one. Wrought iron gates have many gaps that are large enough for a puppy to climb through or, worse still, get his head stuck. Purchasing a rigid, plastic-coated panel is ideal for attaching to the gate and it can be removed once the puppy is fully grown. Now check your plants! Some are toxic to dogs and a quick search on the internet will give you a list of these. You may need to move some plants into your front garden or remove them completely. Planted tubs with colourful bedding plants are an invitation to Bichons to dig them up and shred them. Replace bedding plants with a sturdy shrub or buy pots that are at least 24 in (61 cm) high.

PROOFING YOUR HOME

Puppy proofing your house is equally important. You should think of it in the same way as you would protect a toddler from dangers. Your main area of concern is electric wires, which puppies are attracted to and will chew. Tuck all wires away and if any are exposed, never leave your pup alone. Electrocution is one of the main causes of accidental deaths in puppies.

Get down on your hands and knees (or lower if possible) and view your home from a puppy's perspective. What looks enticing, what is breakable, what is sharp and what do you not want destroyed? You do not want to find that a valuable or treasured heirloom is ruined by teeth marks…

Make sure that a puppy cannot get access to chemicals or dangerous substances typically found under the sink, in your garage, greenhouse or shed. Chocolate is an underestimated

An inquisitive puppy will explore every nook and cranny of his new surroundings.

danger so keep it securely out of reach. A single bar of chocolate could be enough to kill a puppy.

BUYING EQUIPMENT

Before you bring your new arrival home you will want to make a shopping list of everything that your puppy or rescued dog will need. Walking around a large pet shop can be daunting; it is very tempting to buy everything and anything, particularly if it looks cute. Try to keep to the basic requirements. Remember, a puppy can be very destructive and will chew or demolish many unsuitable items. You can always treat your Bichon to lots of goodies when you get to know

what he likes. Some Bichons loathe soft, furry bedding and will opt for a tiled floor every time. Others will jump into a doughnut-shaped bed and be extremely comfortable. Indulgence in luxury is fine, provided the items are safe and suitable for a Bichon.

CRATE

A crate is a very useful item as it can be used as a Bichon's den and rest area. It is somewhere you can leave your dog if you do not want him to have free run of the house. This applies particularly to times when it is not convenient to have him underfoot – for example when guests are arriving, during mealtimes or when you are receiving deliveries. A crate can also be moved easily to your car to provide a safe container while you are driving.

Collapsible wire or hard plastic crates are ideal, virtually indestructible and easily cleaned. This type of crate also has a wire mesh door where you can attach a water bowl. Fabric crates can be more easily destroyed and are harder to clean efficiently. There is also nowhere to attach a water bowl.

Make sure you buy a crate that is large enough to accommodate a full size Bichon. You can block

Most Bichons like to curl up in a small, cosy bed.

off half the crate by placing a box or something similar at the far end. This will stop an initially oversized crate being used as a toilet.

DOG BED AND BEDDING

There is a huge array of dog beds and bedding available. Generally Bichons like to curl up into a smaller rather than oversized one. Padded fabric dogs beds are popular and buying a small one to suit a puppy will give him a cosy, draught-free bed, which will also be ideally suited to placing in his crate if you are going to use one. Be prepared to buy a larger bed once your puppy has grown. Hard, plastic oval-shaped beds are inexpensive and can be lined with a blanket, towel or a padded bed. They are usually slightly raised off the ground, which will prevent spilt water soaking into the bedding and allows healthy air flow.

PLAYPEN OR BABY GATE

A baby gate is useful as you need to restrict your puppy's activities for the first few weeks. If you are restricting the puppy to your kitchen, it is safer to use a baby gate than to open and close a solid door. A puppy will lie beside the door waiting for you to return, and if you cannot see him, opening the door could cause injury. It is also easy to forget to shut a door that you have been used to leaving open, particularly in a busy household. If your downstairs is open plan, you will want a gate at the bottom of the stairs. A playpen is an alternative solution.

FEEDING BOWLS

Feeding bowls come in many shapes, sizes and materials, but stainless steel or ceramic are the best. They both tolerate hot water in the dishwasher and stainless steel is indestructible. Plastic bowls can hold food and

detergent smells and they also scratch easily. It is important to have more than one water bowl. It is easy to close the kitchen door while your puppy has a cuddle with you on the sofa on a hot day and forget he does not have access to water. So make sure you have a water bowl anywhere that your Bichon might be.

Do not forget to put fresh water outside in the shade in hot weather. Again, a stainless steel bowl is a good choice, but a non-spill plastic bowl is practical and very useful in areas where you are likely to trip. Do remember to always keep fresh water in your car. A non-spill bowl can be filled from a water bottle and will be very useful if you find you are stuck in a traffic jam, or if your air conditioning breaks down on the hottest day of the year.

COLLAR AND LEAD

A collar is essential and your puppy should wear one as soon as possible. The market is flooded with a wide range of dog collars from bright-coloured nylon to diamond-encrusted, but consider the size of a Bichon and his coat before making a decision.

A flat, nylon collar is ideal as it is lightweight. A leather collar is also fine but do not get one that is too thick or heavy; it can be uncomfortable and erode the coat from around the neck. 'Jewel'-encrusted collars may look cute and are acceptable for a special occasion, but, in the long term, the coat can get caught in the claws that hold the 'jewels' in place, which will be uncomfortable

The most common and safest dog collar is the buckle type, rather like a belt which can be easily adjusted to adapt to a growing puppy. You must remove the collar from your puppy once a week, not only so that you can groom the coat under the collar, but also because you will be able to adjust it regularly to allow for his rapid growth. Never use a choke chain or collar; they are not suitable for a Bichon. Even with larger dogs choke chains are rarely used correctly and can do more harm than good.

There is a wide variety of collars and leads available in pet stores, but it is best to go for a practical choice.

A rescued dog may have had a bad experience with a collar so a body harness is an ideal soution. A puppy that has walked well on a collar and lead may suddenly start to rebel. This is likely to be due to irritation around the neck glands due to teething around the age of six months. In the short term, the use of a body harness may help until the teething period is over.

There are various leads available but they all clip on to a collar in the same way. You may like to get a retractable extended lead, which gives your Bichon more scope to run around. They should only be used in open spaces where the extended lead will not wrap itself around trees or other obstacles and more importantly will not cause injury to someone who could trip over it. Extended leads are particularly useful for an infirm or aged owner who can give his Bichon plenty of exercise without walking the same distance as the dog.

ID
You should have a collar tag made with your puppy's name and your telephone number engraved on it. This could be purchased in advance of your puppy's arrival. Metal tags are ideal, as the engraving cannot wear out. Plastic tags are more flimsy, and it is best to avoid the type where you insert your dogs information on card or paper into a sleeve rather like a luggage tag, because water could render it illegible. Some puppies come from the breeder with a tattoo, usually found inside the ear. The breeder may have registered your name with the National Tattoo Register or will give you the paperwork to register yourself.

A few Bichon puppies come from the breeder with microchips, or you may want to consider having one inserted when the puppy is older. A rescued dog may have a microchip or tattoo, so be sure to contact the relevant organisation and update it with your name and address.

It is so important to have either an identity tag, tattoo or microchip so that, if your dog is lost, you can be reunited quickly. None of these types of ID are expensive. Having two forms of identity is even better as, in rare cases, identity tags can detach, tattoos can fade and microchips can fail.

GROOMING EQUIPMENT

Grooming equipment is essential to keep your Bichon's coat and skin healthy. The most important tool is a slicker brush. They come in various sizes, some being harder than others. Start your puppy with a 2-in (5-cm) wide slicker brush for around his head and face, and a 3-in (7-cm) brush for his body. Be sure that the slicker is soft.

With an older, rescued Bichon you will need a larger slicker, and, if his coat is quite coarse, you may need to consider a slightly harsher brush. You will also need to buy a comb. It is important to comb through the coat after using the slicker. A comb will find knots close to the skin that a slicker brush may miss. A wide-toothed metal comb will do the job well.

TOYS

Buying toys for your Bichon is fun but try to give a variety, particularly those that will entertain him. A basket full of stuffed, cuddly toys may look cute but is quite boring. A Bichon will usually find one that he likes and ignore the rest. Buy a mix of toys – soft, throw, dental, squeaky and Kongs. Kongs can be used as a toy or be stuffed with treats to keep your dog occupied. Always buy from a reputable pet store and be aware that poorly made, unbranded toys may be dangerous.

CHECK LIST

- Crate
- Bed
- Bedding
- playpen (optional)
- Water and food bowls
- Collar with identity tag and lead
- Slicker and comb
- Variety of toys

CHOOSING A VET

Recommendation is always a good starting point for deciding on a vet. If you live in the country, you may not have any choice but to go to the nearest vet; in a more built-up area you will have choice. Check what arrangements a vet has for out-of-hours emergencies. Larger practices often have a rota of vets on call and you can go to your usual practice where your dog's medical records are at hand. Other vets direct you to a partner practice, but consider the location carefully. You do not want to be driving 30 miles in the dead of night with a sick dog along roads you do not know.

If your pet needs to stay at the vet's surgery overnight, it is worth checking whether someone will

Your puppy will appreciate a variety of different toys.

After all the hard work of rearing a litter, it is time for the puppies to go to their new homes.

be monitoring him continuously. Most vets will make arrangements for this when necessary, although it may involve transferring your pet to another location.

The prices that a veterinary practice charges are not a reliable indication of the quality of care your dog will receive. The cheapest may not be the worst or the most expensive the best. You may well be paying extra for a fancy waiting room with an array of exotic plants! It's a good idea to find out what exactly is included when you are given a quote. Vaccinations may vary with what is included. If your pet is

having an operation, will there be a charge for post-surgery check-up, or for suture removal?

Insurance is an excellent idea, but remember that some practices require payment of fees before your claim is settled. Calling into a vet to make enquiries will give you an idea as to whether the staff are cheerful and helpful.

COLLECTING YOUR BICHON
Every breeder has a different way of getting puppies ready for their new homes but there is a set standard of items you should expect to receive:

- You should be given a pedigree of your puppy showing his parents, grandparents and great-grandparents.
- If the breeder has declared the puppy to be Kennel Club registered, you should be given the puppy's registration papers. Sometimes the breeder may not yet have registered the litter while, for example, he decides on names. In this case you should have a contract that states the puppy will be Kennel Club registered within two months and that the papers will be forwarded to you.

You will need to go through important paperwork before you take your puppy home.

- If you are buying the puppy as a pet/companion some breeders will expect you to neuter your puppy eventually and will withhold their registration document until they see evidence that this has been carried out. This is acceptable provided the conditions are put clearly in writing in the form of a contract.
- You should be made aware of any endorsements that are, or will appear, on your registration. There are two possible endorsements. The first, 'Progeny not eligible for registration', means you may not breed from your puppy, but if you do (which is likely to be a breach of the terms of your contact), you will not be able to register the resulting puppies at the Kennel Club. The second, 'Not eligible for the issue of an Export Pedigree' simply means you may not register your puppy in another country.
- You should also be offered four to six weeks free medical insurance. This may be through the Kennel Club but if you have not received the registration papers you should be given an alternative insurance policy from the breeder.
- Breeders will generally have a litter health-checked by their vet and it is reassuring to see evidence of this.
- You should be given written details of when your puppy was given worming treatment and when his next worming medication is due.
- Any health issues that the puppy may have had must be declared in writing. Without this your insurance could be invalid.
- You should receive a detailed

diet sheet from your breeder, guiding you through a recommended feeding routine from puppy to adulthood and, additionally, receive at least a week's supply of the food that the puppy has been used to.

- Some puppies will have been given their first vaccination, so be sure that you receive their vaccination records. It is not necessary for puppies to have their vaccinations before they are sold if they are under 10 weeks of age, if all other dogs in the home are vaccinated and if the puppies have not been removed from their mother at a very early age. Any puppies purchased from a commercial kennel should be vaccinated.
- You should also receive advice on socialisation, exercise, housetraining, settling your puppy in the first few days, crate training and treatments for flea and tick prevention.
- As a Bichon's coat requires considerable grooming, care and maintenance, you should be given advice on this aspect. Some breeders will give you a puppy's first slicker brush and comb.
- You are likely to be asked to sign a contract of sale. Read through it very carefully and do not hesitate to ask questions if there is anything

CHANGING DIET

It is important that your puppy is fed the diet he is accustomed to for the first week or so. A sudden change of food can cause an upset stomach, which is the last thing you need when you bring your puppy home. Puppies need stability in their diet and a change from one food to another should be done gradually, with the new food increased over a number of days until it is the only food fed. If you are adding anything extra to their diet again do so gradually and in small quantities. If you should change their diet be sure you have a good reason for doing so and do not make any further changes for at least two weeks.

you do not understand. A contract is there to protect you and your puppy, and although it may seem daunting, it is usually a sign that you are buying from a responsible breeder who wishes to set down all conditions or restrictions that apply to the sale of your puppy.

Check the date of birth on all the documents you receive and be sure they are the same. You should not buy a puppy less than eight weeks of age. The care of puppies under this age is very different and should not be attempted by anyone without knowledge and experience. It is the responsibility of a breeder to

raise their puppies, even if orphaned, to an age where they will be mature enough to cope with the demands of moving to a new home.

ADULT BICHONS
Bichons obtained though a rescue organisation may not have been handed in with any documentation at all. The organisation will inform you whether you need to have your dog vaccinated and will give you advice about the health of your Bichon. Very often, the dog will have already have been checked by a vet, vaccinated and neutered.

Should you acquire a Bichon directly from another owner be sure you have all the documentation. If none is forthcoming, you need to check for a microchip or tattoo and receive verification that the previous registered owner is the one that sold or gave away their Bichon. You would have some awkward explaining to do if it was discovered that the dog was stolen! You must then go to a vet as soon as possible for a full health check, flea prevention, worming medication and vaccinations.

CHECK LIST
- Three-generation pedigree
- Kennel Club Registration
- Medical Insurance
- Worming details
- Diet Sheet

- Food
- Vaccination record where applicable
- Written advice on socialisation, exercise, future training, etc
- Identity documentation if applicable
- Coat care advice
- Contract of Sale

MEETING THE FAMILY

It is exciting bringing your puppy home for the first time so make it a good experience for your puppy, too. It is tempting to invite neighbours, family and children to meet your puppy, but this is not a good idea. The first day should be a quiet time so that you can concentrate on your puppy's needs and introduce him to your home and immediate family. It is likely that this is the first time your puppy has been away from his mother and siblings, and will need all the security you can give him. Puppies have bursts of energy followed by long naps and too much excitement with hoards of people around is going to be an overwhelming experience. Let each member of the family have that long-awaited cuddle with the puppy but interspersed with a short burst of play.

Take time introducing the puppy to his new family.

CHILDREN

Supervise children at all times. An over-excited child can easily fall on top of a puppy and a toddler may want to give it a hug and squeeze which could cause serious injury or worse. Setting up a puppy playpen works well with children in the house. It provides a safe haven and it is a good idea to make a rule that only an adult may take the puppy out of the pen. You are then able to supervise play times and can be sure that your new arrival will not be accidentally harmed. Never allow children to pick up the puppy from his bed; the bed is his sanctuary and he should be left to rest undisturbed.

OTHER DOGS

Introducing a new puppy into a home where there is already an established dog needs to handled with a little sensitivity. Your existing dog was there first and he needs to adapt to his new companion. Let him sniff and greet the puppy, and if he seems to be at all put out, you will need to supervise the introduction period for a while. If the adult becomes too boisterous, keep him on a lead for a few days while he gets to know his new companion so you maintain some control. This is particularly important if your older dog is a larger breed.

Do not divert all your attention to the new arrival; your first dog needs attention too. Praise him when he is calm and settled with the puppy and he will understand that this new bundle of white fur is an addition to the family and not a replacement.

OTHER PETS

A cat is likely to keep away from a puppy, but sometimes they mix well and become great friends. It is more likely your cat will be annoyed by your Bichon, who will be expecting it to play on demand. Short, frequent supervised sessions will help them get used to each other. A few hisses usually give a puppy a warning and he will soon learn the boundary between annoyance and companionship!

Do not allow your puppy to chase a cat; it is not fair on your cat and could lead to your Bichon becoming a lifelong, anti-social cat chaser. Make sure your dog does not have access to your cat's litter box. Sooner or later, he may attempt to eat its contents!

SETTLING IN

When you arrive home with your puppy, put him down on the floor and let him explore his new home. Remember to put paper on the floor within easy reach so that he can go to the toilet. If the weather is suitable you may first put him down in the garden.

Initially do not give him free run of the entire house. Your puppy may become confused and forget where you have placed his toilet. He has an entire lifetime to discover every corner of your home, and a puppy does not need to have this experience thrown at him in his first week with you! He has much to get used to: a new house, new smells, change of environment, and new people, which is demanding enough.

Do not carry the puppy around with you; you need to strike a balance between giving your Bichon all the love and affection he demands and allowing him to become a confident, independent dog. Puppies are not babies and if you treat him as one, you will eventually end up with behavioural problems.

The ideal set-up for a puppy is to provide a playpen. There are many types that can be purchased but as you may not need a pen for more than a few months you can easily and cheaply make one up from plastic-coated compost panels available from most garden centres. You may want to revive a no-longer-used child's playpen from your loft. You could find that you have a perfect area such as under the stairs which simply needs a gate. Inside the playpen you can place his crate, water bowl and food. Put newspaper down in an area away from the food and water bowl so that he has somewhere to go to the toilet.

If you do not feel the need for

Give your puppy a chance to explore his new surroundings.

a playpen, ensure that the puppy's bed or crate is in a quiet, draught-free corner away from high-traffic areas. Water should be close by as well as an area of paper. Puppies usually relieve themselves within a minute of waking up and shortly after eating, so it is essential that he can find his 'toilet' quickly.

HOUSE TRAINING

House training is often a worry for first-time dog owners but is really not that difficult. You need to be consistent, structured, attentive and dedicated to the task. If toilet training is carried out correctly from the start, you should have a clean Bichon within six to eight weeks and all your committed efforts will have paid off. Be warned, if you do not put in the effort required, you may set up bad habits that may never be completely broken.

An adult or rescued Bichon may be described as 'house trained' but in a new environment he could regress; therefore, you should treat any new arrival in the same manner as a puppy. If your rescued dog has been neglected in the past, it is important to understand that he could take longer to house train than a puppy; you must firstly undo bad habits and then retrain.

Your aim is to train your puppy to go to the toilet outside, and only if the weather is extreme, to go on paper in an area you choose. A puppy needs to relieve himself a least half a dozen times a day and will always do so

Establish a routine of taking your puppy outside at regular intervals and he will soon learn what is required.

shortly after a nap or after eating. This gives you a perfect window of opportunity to take your puppy outside, as you will not wait long for the desired results. Stay with your puppy, and, as he starts to perform, gently repeat over and over a chosen 'trigger' word. Make sure the word is not his name or one used everyday in your home – you can imagine the results!

Once he has finished give exuberant praise with animation in your voice. Telling him he is a good boy in a flat tone of voice will mean nothing to him. Dogs

understand what you saying more by tone than vocabulary, especially in their early years. Training takes time but continual use of a trigger word will come into its own when the puppy matures. It is very useful to condition a dog to relieve himself before a long journey or on a bitterly cold night. Remember to put your puppy outside so that you minimise the chance of an accident.

A puppy is unable to go through the night without needing to go to the toilet. Whether he is in a pen or a

confined area such as
your kitchen you must
provide paper. Start with a
large area of paper so that
it is difficult for him to
miss the mark. That area
can slowly be reduced in
size. Never put a puppy in
a closed crate at night
until he is four to five
months of age. He will
have no choice but to
relieve himself in or
around his bed, which
will make for a very
unhappy Bichon. If you
are using a crate never put
paper in the crate; you
will be asking him to be
dirty on or around his
sleeping area, which will
totally confuse him and set up an
undesirable habit which will be
very difficult to break.

It is useful to have an area that
you can chose to cover with paper
so that your Bichon can relieve
himself. Most breeds of dog can
relieve themselves outside but
with small breeds – and
particularly those with high-
maintenance coats, such as a
Bichon – there are times that you
will not want him to go outside.
Torrential rain or heavy snow are
not ideal conditions, particularly
late at night. You will not want to
put a cold, wet, dirty dog to bed
and it is at times like this that a
paper area comes into its own.

Your puppy is bound to have
accidents initially, particularly
when startled or over-excited.
Dogs like to go back to a spot
where they have previously
urinated, so it is essential to mop

ACCIDENTS WILL HAPPEN

Do not scold your puppy for accidents;
it will achieve nothing, particularly
after the event. If your puppy happily
greets you as you notice the accident and
you tell him off, he will think he was scolded
for greeting you. You can now see how easy
it is to confuse a dog! Think calmly and
logically – more behavioural problems are
down to an owner than a dog.

up, particularly carpet. Urine
smells are most effectively
removed with bicarbonate of
soda. If he urinates away from his
toilet area, soak up any urine
with paper and place on top of
the paper area you have set up.
Your puppy will more likely seek
out this spot next time.

With constant vigilance you
will get to know when your
puppy is about to relieve himself,
and, combined with his
increasing ability to control his
bladder, you should end up with
a well-trained dog.

THE FIRST NIGHT
For his first night your puppy
should be put where he is to
sleep every night, most
commonly in the kitchen. Do not
make the mistake of leaving a
light on 'in case he gets
frightened in the dark'. A dark

room entices a dog to
sleep. It will also stop him
exploring while
unsupervised if left in a
room without a pen. You
may find that he starts to
howl and cry, and some
puppies are more
stubborn than others.
Even though it seems
harsh, he is better left
alone for the night and for
you to weather the storm.
The puppy will soon tire
and fall asleep. If you keep
checking up on him he
will quickly learn to get
attention by howling.
Bichons may be small and
cute but they are also
intelligent.

EARLY LEARNING
Your puppy is going to be
introduced to many new
experiences. It is vitally important
that each experience is a good
one and any teaching should be
fun. Praise and reward are the two
things to remember; punishment
is proven to be ineffective and
confusing. For example, if your
puppy should run away, it would
be senseless to scold him when
he returns. He would connect the
scolding with his return, not
running away! It is unwise to call
him to you to punish him, as he
will soon learn not to respond
when you call his name.

HANDLING
The breeder should have made a
head start in socialising your
puppy. Hopefully he has been
handled by other people, which

HANDLING YOUR PUPPY

Your puppy needs to get used to being handled all over so that he accepts grooming and examination by a vet when required.

Gently restrain your puppy until he relaxes.

Lift the ear-flap and check inside the ears.

Part the lips to examine the teeth and gums.

Lift each paw in turn.

Work your way along the body, remembering to praise your puppy for his co-operation.

MOUTHING

If you watch a litter of puppies playing, you will notice that they spend much of their time biting and grabbing each other with their mouths. When you take a puppy from the litter, the puppy will play-bite and mouth you instead of his siblings. This is normal behaviour but, as the puppy gets older, his jaw strengthens and a play-bite will soon become a hard bite. You need to teach a puppy bite inhibition from an early age.

Every time the puppy touches you with his teeth, say "Ouch!" in a harsh tone of voice. This will probably not stop the puppy from mouthing, but over time should result in softer and gentler puppy biting. The commands necessary to teach a puppy not to mouth are easy and fun. Hold a small handful of the puppy's dry food, say "Take it" and give the puppy one piece of food. Then close the rest of the food in your hand and say "Off". When the puppy has not touched your hand for three to five seconds, say "Take it" and give the puppy one piece of food. You are teaching the puppy that "Off" means not to touch. Repeat this exercise frequently over two or three months; its fun and you will be preventing play-biting developing into unacceptable behaviour.

will make the transition to his new human family much easier. Try to get a puppy to come towards you before you pick him up and do not make sudden movements when doing so; it can startle a puppy that will associate jumping out of his skin with being picked up. Hold a puppy securely with two hands: one under the chest and the other supporting the dog's rear end. Do not let him scamper over your shoulder. It is a long way down if he misjudges his climbing ability. Never pick him up by his neck and always demonstrate to children the correct way to lift a dog.

Try training your puppy to stand up by supporting him between his front and back legs.

After two or three seconds give him praise and a treat. Gradually extend the time he will stand for you. This is good basic training for when he is to be groomed or for visits to the vet.

WEARING A COLLAR

Collars should be introduced to your puppy right away. Do not be concerned if he initially scratches at it or shakes his head. Though he may resist wearing a collar, soon he will not even notice it is on. Taking the time to properly introduce your puppy to the collar and, later, to the lead, sets the stage for teaching him the basic elements of obedience. The goal is to have your puppy accept a collar and lead calmly, without resisting, and to look forward to

many years of walks with you. *For more information on lead walking, see Chapter Six: Training and Socialisation.*

CAR TRAVEL

Your puppy's first experiences riding in a car will influence his future reactions to being taken for a car ride. Fortunately, owners can take steps to prevent or reduce their puppy's stress and fear. For the first few days or so, introduce your puppy to the car by putting him inside, praising him, and offering him a small meal or a few treats, then taking him back out of the vehicle. Once your puppy appears comfortable being put in the car, turn the engine on while he plays with a new toy or just sits on your lap (or in his crate) in the back seat.

Once your puppy feels confident being in the car while the engine is running, begin taking your puppy for short, pleasant daily car rides, preferably in his crate or in a puppy safety seat. Once or twice around the block will suffice. Despite all your efforts some dogs will be car sick. Your vet should be able to give you medication to help and there are several herbal remedies that have proved effective. Car sickness is usually something a puppy will outgrow.

Always make sure your is dog contained (this is where the use of a crate comes into its own) or restrained with a harness attached to a seat belt. It is extremely dangerous to let a puppy loose in your car; he could end up under your feet preventing you using your brake, and will be a serious distraction.

Accustom your puppy to travelling in a carrier where he will be safe and secure.

THE BEST OF CARE

5

Chapter

When you take on a Bichon Frisé, you are responsible for his needs for the duration of his life. This includes feeding him the correct diet, exercising him, and grooming him.

DIET AND NUTRITION

To begin with, we will look at the various types of diet available on the market today, along with the relevance to each life stage of your dog. Whichever type of diet is selected, it is essential to provide proper nutrition for the maintenance of optimum health and activity throughout your dog's life. Failure to provide an adequately nutritional diet may result in disease and sub-optimal activity and development as our dogs grow, mature and age.

The food we provide for our dogs, in addition to providing specific nutrients, must also supply sufficient energy – a fundamental requirement of all animals, providing the power for cells to function. Energy is provided in the diet from carbohydrates, fats and protein; the amounts of each in a food determines its energy content. Dietary fat alone provides approximately twice as much energy as carbohydrate and protein combined. It can be seen, therefore, that fat is a more efficient fuel for metabolism and the importance of high-energy constituents in some life stages of our dogs.

Protein, fat and carbohydrate are known as macronutrients and, along with dietary fibre, are the main nutritional providers.

PROTEIN

Proteins are large molecules made up an infinite number of the different 20 amino acids linked together by peptide bonds. Each protein chain, therefore, has its own characteristic properties.

Protein is an essential component of living cells where they regulate metabolism and play a structural role in living tissue and muscle fibre. It can be seen, therefore, that the protein constituent of any diet is important for tissue growth and repair. It is a constituent essential for a 'growth' diet or high-energy diet, and during periods of pregnancy, lactation and when repair of body tissues is required, but is needed in lesser quantity in senior diets. Your Bichon Frisé need a good-quality source of dietary protein to provide the essential amino acids that cannot be synthesised by the body in sufficient amounts for optimum performance and growth. Non-essential amino acids, although of equal importance, can be synthesised from excess of other amino acids.

Growing puppies need a high level of protein in their diet.

Animal proteins generally have a more balanced amino acid with better digestibility than plant proteins, providing protein of higher biological value (the proportion of protein that can be utilised by the body). Dietary protein taken in excess to the body's requirement is converted to fat and stored as adipose tissue. It can therefore be seen how easily a dog can become obese if a diet containing an excess of protein is fed. Likewise, a diet deficient in protein can cause poor growth or weight loss, rough and dull coat, anorexia, muscle wasting and, in extreme cases, death due to an increased susceptibility to disease.

FAT
Dietary fat consists of a mixture of triglycerides, each being a combination of three fatty acids joined together by glycerol bonds, which gives each fat its own characteristic. Fatty acids are described as saturated (where there are no double bonds between atoms) or unsaturated (where one or more double bonds are present). Unsaturated fat is further catorgerised into monounsaturated fats, which contain one double bond, and polyunsaturated, which contain more than one double bond. Most fats contain all types of fat but in a wide variety of proportions.

Fat serves as the most concentrated source of energy in a diet and provides palatability and texture to food. Its main function is to provide essential fatty acids that cannot be synthesised in the body, and as a carrier for the fat-soluble vitamins A, D, E and K. There are currently three known essential

Carbohydrates provide the body with energy.

fatty acids, all polyunsaturated – linoleic, a-linolenic and arachidonic acids. These essential fatty acids are involved in many aspects of a dog's health, including kidney and reproduction function, and are essential components of all cell membranes. Deficiency can result in poor coat and skin quality, anaemia and fertility problems.

CARBOHYDRATE

Carbohydrate provides the body with energy and may be converted to fat. Carbohydrates include simple sugars, such as glucose, and the complex sugars, such as starch, which consist of chains of the simple sugars. All animals have a requirement for glucose, but providing the diet contains the glucose precursors

(amino acids and glycerol), most can synthesise enough to meet their metabolic requirements without the need for dietary intake.

DIETARY FIBRE

Dietary fibres are indigestible polysaccharides such as cellulose, pectin and lignin. These materials generally escape digestion and pass straight through the digestive tract. A limited amount in the diet provides bulk to the faeces, regulating bowel movements and thus preventing diahorrea and constipation.

TYPES OF DIET

Many types of diet are now available widely on the pet food market. Each dog may be suited to a different type of diet, and

observation of the health, condition and bodyweight of your Bichon will determine whether adjustments are required.

PREPARED FOODS

The vast majority of dogs in developed countries are fed on commercially prepared foods. These foods are convenient, nutritionally balanced and can be purchased in a variety of flavours and textures. There are three main types of food available:

- **Dry Foods:** These include 'complete' diets, which provide a balanced diet when fed alone, and biscuits that are fed in combination with an additional food. Complete diets are normally a mixture of dry, flaked or crushed cereals

Moist diets are appetising, but they have a high moisture content.

The 'dry' or 'complete' diet caters for all your Bichon's nutritional needs.

Feeding an all-meat diet is not recommended.

and vegetables, and include a meat-based, dry protein concentrate. Biscuits are usually made from wheaten flour. Dry foods have moisture content of 10-14 per cent.

- **Moist Foods:** These diets are packed in cans, plastic or foil containers. They tend to have a higher meat content and are generally packed in jelly/gravy mixtures, improving palatability. Moist foods do, however, have moisture content of 60-85 per cent.
- **Semi-moist Foods:** These are composed of meat and cereal mixtures which is cooked to a paste and extruded into pieces. This diet has a moisture content of 25-40 per cent.

HOME PREPARED DIETS

Some people prefer to feed fresh foods prepared at home. However, this must provide a formulation that is balanced and takes into account the dog's lifestage, the nutritional value of the foodstuffs used and the methods and convenience of preparing and storing. Considerable time and expertise is required to be able to offer the dog a consistent and nutritionally balanced diet.

- **Meat:** Lean meat is a poor source of calcium, and feeding an all-meat diet can cause nutritional diseases such as secondary hyperparathyroidism (a disease caused by calcium deficiency or phosphorus excess where calcium is absorbed from bone, causing lameness and pain).
- **Fish:** Care should be taken when feeding raw fish as this can lead to thiamine deficiency in prolonged feeding. Large amounts of oily fish can cause a deficiency of Vitamin E. However, a small quantity of cooked fish can provide a valuable protein source.
- **Eggs:** These provide good-quality protein, but should be fed cooked to destroy avidin (which binds biotin, a valuable B Vitamin).
- **Milk, Cheese And Dairy:** These are a good source of protein, fat, calcium and phosphorus. However, some animals may be intolerant to lactose.
- **Cereals And Vegetables:** These should be cooked to aid digestibility, but provide a good source of dietary fibre.

Cooking is generally considered advisable, but many people choose to feed some components raw. It should be noted that cooking meat will kill most bacteria and parasites and improve digestibility. Over-cooking should be avoided, as this destroys valuable vitamins. Home diets will generally require some nutritional supplementation.

FEEDING FOR DIFFERENT LIFESTAGES

Feeding your Bichon through the different stages of his life must provide all the nutritional differences required at different stages.

PUPPY, PREGNANCY & LACTATION

In relation to bodyweight, these stages require a much-increased intake nutritionally. Puppies require not only sufficient nutrition for maintenance but also rapid growth. As with pregnancy and lactation, the dog has higher demands for energy, protein, and the minerals calcium and phosphorous. Dietary deficiencies at this stage can cause growth and skeletal developmental problems in puppies, and illness and emaciation in the pregnant/lactating bitch. The requirement of protein in the diet fed should be 22-28 per cent; fat should be 30-50 per cent, fibre 5 per cent.

Diets should provide concentrated food, as the dog has to eat a large quantity relative to his size, so the daily feed should therefore be split into several meals. Excessive energy intake should be avoided as this can lead to obesity and illness in the pregnant and lactating bitch, and in puppies can lead to skeletal abnormalities, as the bones develop at the incorrect rate and/or obesity in later life.

Puppies: At weaning (six to eight weeks) puppies' requirements are about double those of an adult. As the dog grows and matures, this requirement falls. By the time a puppy reaches 40 per cent of his adult weight, he requires 1.6 times the adult requirement, and at 80 per cent he requires only 1.2 times. While high levels of good-quality protein are required for growth, in excess it is stored as fat.

Growth diets should be fed until at least 75 per cent of the adult weight is attained, with the daily food requirement split into four or five smaller meals. If complete diets are fed, extra supplementation should not be required. If a home-prepared diet

Following weaning, a puppy needs four meal a day.

regime is followed, supplementation may be required to ensure an adequate balance is achieved. By approximately 10 weeks of age, the frequency of meals can be reduced, and, by around five months, feeding twice daily is recommended, allowing the puppy to utilise the energy provided more efficiently.

By the time puppies go to their new homes at approximately eight weeks, they should be eating a well-balanced puppy diet. This diet should be continued for the first few weeks to allow acclimitisation to a new environment and to ensure the puppy eats well away from a litter. If the new owner wishes to change the diet due to personal preference, this should be done gradually over a period of at least a couple of weeks. Any sudden changes in diet can cause gastrointestinal upset.

Pregnancy/Lactation: While an increased nutritional diet is required, over-feeding should be avoided, particularly in early pregnancy, as this can predispose to problems during whelping. Milk production is affected by protein quality, so good, highly digestible protein must be provided. A gradual increase in nutritional requirement is needed over the second half of gestation, starting with 15 per cent of the bitch's ration, increasing to 60 per cent the week before whelping. At peak lactation, when the puppies are growing rapidly, the bitch must be provided with nutrition to support herself and a litter. She may need up to four times her normal requirement.

Maintenance: A maintenance diet is considered to be necessary when your Bichon has reached

When a bitch is feeding puppies her nutritional needs are at their highest.

When feeding an adult, it is advisable to split rations between two meals a day.

his full adult size and weight, and there are no additional energy requirements placed on him. Adult dogs require 16-20 per cent protein, 30-50 per cent fat, and 5 per cent fibre. Excess protein and fat is laid down as adipose tissue and causes the animal to become obese. Most adult dogs can survive on a diet of vegetable material, however a diet containing animal protein would provide more appropriate nutrition.

Most adult dogs can be fed on a once-daily feeding regime. However, it is often more appropriate to feed twice a day, to allow the animal to evacuate his bowels and to allow for more effective utilisation of the energy derived from the diet.

Senior Animals: Animals are generally considered to be senior when they are in the last third of their expected lifespan. As our dogs age, many will suffer from clinical disease and the diet may have to be altered for that reason. For example, animals with renal disease will require a considerably less protein-rich diet; a dog with cardiac disease will require a diet reduced in sodium. The diet should therefore be altered accordingly.

As dogs age, their activity levels decline and therefore their energy requirements are less; their energy requirement is approximately 20 per cent less than younger adults. Therefore, these elderly patients require a much less calorie-dense diet to compensate. Obesity is a common problem in older dogs, as their diet remains the same but their requirements alter. This, in turn, can lead to further clinical deterioration of an existing disease or produce further illness.

OBESITY
Obesity is the most common form of malnutrition. It is estimated that over 50 per cent of our dogs are overweight, with approximately 25 to 33 per cent clinically obese. As well as obesity reducing the dog's quality of life, it can cause/increase the incidence of numerous medical conditions, including:
• Osteoarthritis
• Respiratory distress
• Reduced exercise intolerance
• Diabetes mellitus

The responsible owner should keep his Bichon lean and healthy.

Photo: John Hartley.

lesser quantity is not recommended. This diet is balanced for normal energy intake and essential nutrients may be lost if the energy intake is reduced. A more effective method is to feed a prepared and balanced low-calorie food formulated for weight reduction.

Obesity is a long term management commitment and one that must be undertaken with this in mind. It will require changes for both dog and owner, as well as a degree of perseverance and patience. It is, however, a commitment we owe to our dogs and is worth the effort for the increase in the quality of life it brings to our pets.

EXERCISE

Bichons do not need a lot of exercise, especially when they are puppies. While their bones are still growing it is imperative they are not over walked. Several short walks a day of, perhaps, 10 to 15 minutes each, extending to maybe half an hour, or at the very most an hour, when they are adults. Puppies need play times when they can interact with the rest of the household. Make sure you let your dogs off the lead only when you are in a secure area, as Bichons are escape artists and will vanish under a fence or between bushes at the first opportunity. They should be exercised on concrete (to help wear down their nails) and grass. If they are walked over the beach on pebbles, this will tighten the muscles in the feet and legs. As

- Circulatory problems
- Cardiac disease
- Renal/Hepatic Disease
- Lower resistance to infection
- Dermatological problems
- Increased surgical and anaesthetic risk
- Increased chance of growths/tumours/lipomas.

Obesity is caused when the energy requirement of the dog is less than that provided by the diet. This results in the deposition of fat in adipose tissue and is associated with fat cell size in adult dogs and fat cell numbers in growing diets (hyperplasia). Once hyperplasia has occurred, the dog will have a life-long predisposition for excessive weight. The importance of correct nutrition at the puppy stage can now be seen.

A dog is considered obese if his bodyweight is 15 per cent or more above the ideal. Practical assessment of the dog's condition can determine obesity, by observing weight, appearance and palpation of the subcutaneous fat deposits. In normal adult dogs, the ribs should just be palpable with a definite waistline.

Dietary therapy is the most effective management of the obese dog, accompanied by an increased exercise regime if appropriate. Dietary management aims to provide moderate controlled energy restriction. Initially a target weight of 15 per cent reduction should be aimed for. For dogs this degree of weight loss can be observed in 12 weeks if 40 to 50 per cent of the dog's energy requirement for maintenance of his target weight is fed.

Feeding a normal diet in a

If you can find a safe area, your Bichon will relish the opportunity for a free run.

they get older you will find that a run round the garden will be plenty for them, but short walks should always be encouraged to keep up their muscle tone and stamina.

GROOMING YOUR BICHON

It is very important to accustom your puppy to being groomed as soon as he arrives in his new home. Time spent grooming your puppy helps you to bond and gives the puppy his special time with you. You also need to think of the future – as your Bichon gets older, you will need to spend a lot of time grooming if you want him to look his best.

PUPPY CARE

You will need a slicker brush, pin brush and a metal comb. If you do not have a grooming table,

you will need to get a rubber mat to put on a work surface. For safety's sake, the dog must be on a non-slip surface when he is being groomed. When you first acquire your puppy, his coat will be very short, but it will still need attention. Give him a gentle brush with the pin brush to start with, so he gets used to being handled and groomed.

The coat should be brushed in both directions and then combed through to make sure there are no knots starting. The coat should be lightly trimmed every four to six weeks to encourage the correct adult coat. As your puppy gets older you will notice the gradual change in the coat. Sometimes a Bichon will appear to have holes in the coat; this is where the puppy coat has shed and the new,

tighter, curled adult coat is beginning to appear. This can happen anytime from four months of age and often coincides with the puppy losing his puppy teeth. You will need to trim off long, wispy bits of coat.

As the Bichon has an undercoat, it is imperative that the puppy is groomed every other day as the full coat starts to appear. It is as at this stage that knots and mats can appear if the coat is neglected. If your Bichon gets wet, you will need to groom him thoroughly as the undercoat, when wet, can become like cotton-wool and mat tightly to the skin; this can be very difficult to tease apart when dry. It is at this time that you must make sure you can get through the coat with your comb without coming up against any knots.

PUPPY CARE

The breeder will give a puppy his first trim.

To begin with work through the coat with a slicker brush.

You can then use a wide-toothed metal comb on the coat.

If your Bichon develops a mat, the best plan is to spray it with a quality conditioner. Then, gently tease the mat apart with your fingers, brush with the slicker brush and finally comb through. You will find that the most frequent areas to mat up are under the front legs (armpits), between the rear legs, and behind the ears. After exercising your Bichon, you may find that the feet, and, in particular, the back hocks, will have a few knots.

ADULT CARE
Adult dogs need extra attention, especially if you like to leave the coat longer than half an inch. Many owners prefer to have a pet cut, which is roughly half an inch all over the body and legs, with just the head, ears and tail left long. This is the most popular trim for a Bichon; some groomers use clippers, rather then scissors, on the body, depending on how short you want the body coat to be.

Other variations on the trim include:
• The poodle cut, where the coat is left longer on the legs, and the paws are clipped almost bare.
• All the coat – even the head – is only left about half an inch all over. with just the tail left long.

Even if you opt for a pet trim, you will still need to set time apart for regular grooming sessions. There will be times when the coat under the ears and chin will get particularly matted. If your pet is allowed to run in the fields, all sorts of dirt can get caught in this part of the coat, so you much be extra vigilant and careful when grooming this area.

ROUTINE CARE
When you are grooming your Bichon, take the opportunity to check him all over to ensure he has no lumps, bumps, or sore areas. You should also check for the presence of external parasites such as fleas or ticks (see page 133). This is essential in a long-coated breed, as it easy to miss

Some pet owners prefer to clip the coat for easy maintenance.

the onset of a problem. Remember, the sooner you spot a problem, the quicker and easier it will be to resolve.

TEETH

Your dog should have his teeth cleaned on a regular basis. When your puppy first arrives in his new home, you can get him used to this procedure by rubbing his gums and baby teeth with your finger with a bit of dog toothpaste on it. As the dog gets older there are many different dental utensils available that will make it easy to keep your dog's teeth and gums in good health. There are also dental chews on the market which can help prevent the build-up of tartar.

NAILS

You will need to check your Bichon's nails on a regular basis to ensure they do not grow too long. There are two kinds of nail clippers, i.e. guillotine and scissor, but you must be very careful not to cut the quick (where the pink bit of the nail starts), as this will result in bleeding and discomfort for your Bichon.

EYES

Your Bichon's eyes need to be checked and cleaned on a regular basis. Some Bichons produce a mucous substance in their eyes and will therefore need them washed every day. There are several products that can be purchased from pet shops to assist in the cleansing of the eyes, and for the prevention or removal of tear staining. Unfortunately, they don't always work, but if applied as directed on a regular basis, they should prevent any build-up of staining and keep the eyes clear and healthy.

There are also some paste products on the market that can be applied to the coat, just under the eye, to stop any further staining. This is particularly useful if you intend to show your Bichon. These products can be purchased from the breed clubs, or you can make a paste yourself by using equal amounts of boric acid powder, or white Fuller's Earth or Kaolin, and cornflour, mixed together with water.

71

ROUTINE CARE

If you keep your Bichon in full coat, he will need regular brushing with a slicker brush.

You will also need to work through the coat with a wide-toothed comb.

The teeth must be cleaned to prevent the build-up of tartar.

EARS

The breeder should have given your puppy his first bath and trim and, hopefully, will have shown you how to pluck the excess fluff from his ears. When you get your puppy home, it is a good idea to fondle his ears when you are giving him a cuddle so that he gets used to them being touched.

It is very important to keep the fluff to a minimum in the ears, as if it is left, it can block the air from circulating in the ear canal and allow infection to manifest. You can pluck the hair from the ears by using your finger and thumb, grasping a few hairs and pulling them towards you. Never remove all the hair, as, should there ever be a problem with infection, it will need the hair to move out of the ear.

BATHING

When it is time to bath your Bichon, it is important to make sure you have groomed the coat thoroughly and ensured there are no knots or mats before getting him wet. You will need to use a good-quality dog shampoo and you must make sure you rinse the coat thoroughly. It is much easier to use a shower attachment when washing your Bichon, as it is then easier to rinse the dog.

If you are washing your Bichon frequently, you can use a conditioner every now and then, but, once again, the coat must be thoroughly rinsed, as any residue left in the coat could set off a skin irritation.

You can towel-dry your dog's coat lightly by patting the dog. Do not rub vigorously as this can cause matting of the coat. You should then groom through the

coat and either leave to dry naturally or preferably dry with a hairdryer, continually brushing the coat out, away from the skin, to give the desired fluffy appearance. It is best to use your slicker brush when doing this. Never hold the dryer too close to the dog and only have on a medium temperature, as you do not want to scald the skin.

If you are drying your dog for show presentation, it is very important to dry the coat in stages. Dry one part of the coat at a time, keeping the rest of the coat damp, either by wrapping it in a damp towel, or by using a water spray to dampen each area as you get to it. It is far more difficult to trim a curly, uneven coat than a well-dried straighter coat.

Your Bichon is living in your home, so you will want him to

Nails will need to be trimmed, taking care not to cut into the quick.

Wipe the eyes to prevent staining and the build-up of debris.

Hair needs to be plucked from inside the ear canal, and ears also need to be wiped clean.

smell nice and look good, even if you are not exhibiting him in the show ring. Obviously, it is entirely up to you how often you bathe him, but maybe plan on a weekly bath, unless he is in the fields every day and comes back home covered in mud. If you have been out in the rain with your Bichon, it is a good idea to gently towel-dry him, groom him through and then dry him off with the hairdryer. Show dogs have to be bathed before every show and, often, in between times. A Bichon's coat must look immaculate; staining on the coat is often heavily penalised.

TRIMMING

Now your Bichon is fluffy and clean, you can tidy up the coat. When trimming, remember that all parts of the Bichon are rounded – nothing is flat or square. If you are hoping to show your puppy, you will no doubt have made enquiries and found someone in your area who can either teach you how to trim your Bichon or do it for you. In the long run you will save yourself a lot of money if you can trim your dog yourself, but it is not something you can learn overnight and the best 'finish' on a coat can take years.

The Breed Standard states: "the dog may be presented untrimmed or have the muzzle and feet slightly tidied up". However, to show your Bichon nowadays you will see they are heavily trimmed. In most countries, the custom is to shape the Bichon to show off his best features, but in France they have to be shown in a natural coat. In the UK, we show our Bichons with as straight a coat as possible,

SAFETY CHECK

It is very important that during the process of bathing and trimming your dog, he is never left on his own. So if the phone rings or the door bell goes, either wrap the dog up and take him with you or ignore it! There have been so many instances of a accidents happening because a dog tried to get out the bath or jumped down off the table while 'Mum' answered the door or the phone, so please do not leave your Bichon alone in the bath or on his grooming table.

even though the Standard calls for the coat to fall naturally in loose curls. In America the trimming is even more exaggerated and they often trim their dogs with very short legs, although recently this has started to change.

Dogs used to be shown with a coat that was 2 to 3 inches (5 to 7 cm) in length, with ear leathers left to grow as long as possible. However, in recent years a more sculptured appearance has been preferred. The ear leathers have been cut to match the beard, and the head overall has a rounded appearance instead of the old bell shape.

The Breed Standard calls for minimum trimming but, in reality, this is rarely adhered to in the show ring, and presentation is of the highest calibre.

Photo: Carol Ann Johnson.

EQUIPMENT

Good quality scissors are essential. Most groomers prefer scissors with 7- or 8-inch (17 to 20-cm) blades, but there are very many types and shapes so should be able to find a pair that you are comfortable with. To start with, just purchase a reasonably priced pair and get used to the feel of them before you start looking at the more expensive ones. There are scissors made for left-handed users as well as right-handed, and the weight of the scissors can very considerably which is why it is so important to try before you buy.

STEP BY STEP

When starting to trim your Bichon, always remember that least is best. Just trim a little at a time and gradually follow the shape of your Bichon. If you are going to attempt to trim your dog yourself, find a good picture of a Bichon and try to copy the trim. There is no substitute for practice, the more you try to do it the easier it will get.

- Use your trimming scissors facing downward when trimming the legs, as this will make it less likely that you take too much off at once. The hair from between the pads should be trimmed out and you should round off the foot. The back legs are more difficult, as you have to be careful to follow the line of the dog's construction, rounding it off

over the rump but not cutting in too short on the second thigh, just before the hock. You need to leave a reasonable amount of hair on the back of the hock; the front of the rear leg needs to follow the bend of stifle. Depending on the efficiency of the trimmer, show dogs can be make to look as if they have wonderful angulation when, in fact, they have been quite straight in stifle.

- When you are trimming the body, keep your scissors parallel with the part of the body you are trimming. You should support your dog's head while attempting to trim the body to keep him still so that you can get a level top line and then go round the body. Sometimes it is easier to start from the base of the tail, trimming towards the neck and then go down the sides and round the body. Be careful not to point your scissors inwards as you will remove too much coat at one time. You must keep lifting the coat with your comb at regular intervals. You must be very careful round your pet's private parts as these areas should be kept quite short and should be trimmed regularly.

- From the body you will then

TRIMMING

Point the scissors downwards when trimming the legs.

Work down the leg and then trim around the foot.

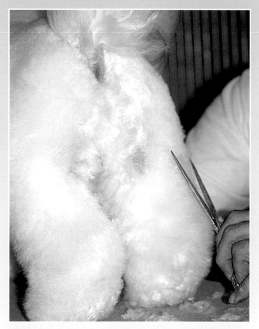

When trimming the hindlegs, follow the line of the dog's construction.

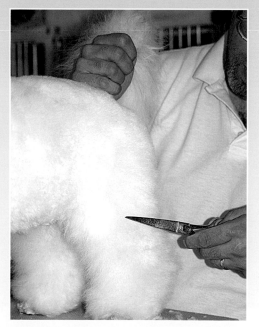

You need to leave a reasonable amount of hair on the back of the hock.

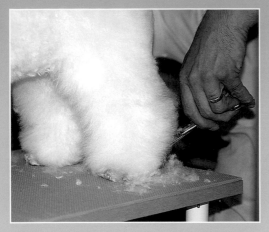

Work down the leg and then round off the foot.

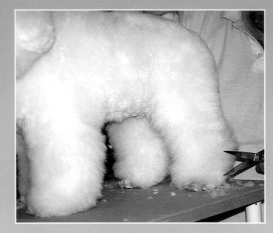

It is easy to see how trimming can influence outward appearance, enhancing a dog's natural construction.

You will need to trim along the topline.

The neck coat is left longer in a show trim.

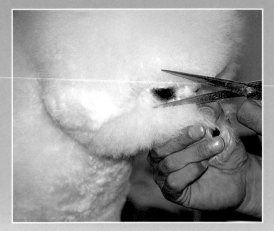

Take great care trimming round the eyes.

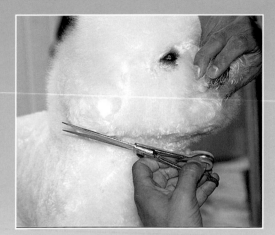

Trim the hair evenly.

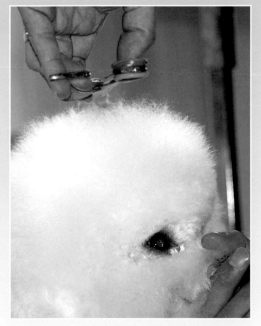

The aim is to for the head to be ball-shaped.

The hair between the pads needs to be trimmed with scissors or you can use clippers.

have to gently trim up the neck stopping just under the ears. Do not forget that the neck will narrow as it gets closer to the head. The neck coat is always left longer in show trims. The chest area should be lightly trimmed to match the rest of the body and tampered into the front legs.

• When you are trimming the head, which can be extremely difficult to do, you must be even more careful how you hold your scissors – the last thing you want to do is poke your dogs eyes out. It may be best to start with round-nosed scissors and then, once you have gained confidence, you can progress to your normal scissors. If you are unable to do a full trim, you should attempt to at least keep your dog's eyes clear. For this, use round-nosed scissors to trim excess hair from the corner of the eyes. Then, use your trimming scissors to round the hair above the eyes to meet with the rest of the coat.

The Bichon head forms a natural ball shape with the equilateral triangle of the eyes and nose forming the central part. The remaining hair should be in equal parts above and below these features, so try to trim it evenly, incorporating the ears. Sometimes, especially with pet trims, the hair above and below the facial features is cut very short and then the ears left long. This is totally unacceptable for a show Bichon. The stained hair around the mouth and eyes should be trimmed away using your round-nosed scissors.

• You will also need to use your round-nosed scissors to trim the excess hair from between the pads. If this is allowed to grow excessively it can become clogged with dirt/chewing gum and any other muck found on the streets. If this is allowed to happen, the dog's pads can become infected. In extreme cases where dirt has been allowed to build up, it can even deform the feet.

• The tail should never be trimmed, only tidied very slightly at the base.

GROWING OLD

As your Bichon gets older, you may find that he will not want to go out as often. He may suddenly want more food or go off his food – neither is unusual – but it is always best to get your dog checked by a vet to make sure it is nothing more than the ageing process.

Your Bichon's coat will change, some more than others, but it will loose density and can become coarse in texture. This is common, and there is very little,

The needs of your Bichon will change as he grows older.

if anything, that can be done, as it is just a natural progression. Not all breeding lines are the same so the degree of change can vary considerably. You should be able to get some idea of how your dog's coat will progress by talking to his breeder.

A Bichon's teeth can start to deteriorate from the age of seven but, again, this can vary depending on breeding lines and also the diet he has been fed. Regular care of the teeth from puppyhood onwards will certainly pay off as your Bichon reaches his senior years.

As with humans, many older dogs develop cataracts, so if you suspect this is happening, consult your vet. Most dogs cope with losing part of their sight very well, just so long as you don't move the furniture, or take them somewhere new…

LETTING GO

It is very hard when a much-loved pet becomes seriously ill, but you must remember all the good times you have had with him and try not to let him suffer. Your vet will be able to tell you if your dog is in pain or not, but only you will know whether your Bichon still has a good quality of life. Medication can be extremely costly and, if it is not improving the quality of your dog's life, it

In time, you will be able to look back and remember all the happy times you spent with your beloved Bichon.

is time to consider saying goodbye. Only you know when the time is right, but try to make the correct decision for your pet's wellbeing – not your own dread of being without him. It is never an easy decision but no one else will make it for you. Of course you will miss your Bichon dreadfully, but in time you will be able to look back and remember all the happy times you spent together, in the full knowledge that you were a caring owner right up to the end.

TRAINING AND SOCIALISATION

Chapter 6

When you decided to bring a Bichon Frisé into your life, you probably had dreams of how it was going to be, spending time with one of the most glamorous of all dogs with the added bonus of personality plus. This sums up the Bichon – but he does not come in a ready-made package. This is an exuberant and fun-loving breed, and these characteristics can make him the perfect pet, or a dog that is wilful and difficult to live with.

It is essential to remember that, for the most part, you will get what you deserve. A Bichon, regardless of whether he is a puppy or an adult, does not come into your home with perfect manners, understanding exactly what you want and fitting perfectly into your lifestyle. A Bichon has to learn his place in your family and he must discover what is acceptable behaviour.

We have a great starting point in that the Bichon Frisé has an outstanding temperament. The breed has been valued throughout the centuries for the very special companionship he gives, and for the way he tunes in with his human family. Quick thinking and highly intelligent, there are times when a Bichon may try to get one step ahead, but, generally, he want to please you. This biddable side to his character, coupled with his ability to engage with people, are the building blocks to producing a well-behaved dog that is a pleasure to live with. Praise and reward your Bichon for good behaviour, and he will thrive on the attention. He wants nothing more than to be with you; the secret is to form a close bond so that pleasing you is his top priority.

THE FAMILY PACK

Dogs have been domesticated for some 14,000 years, but, luckily for us, they have inherited and retained behaviour from their distant ancestor – the wolf. A Bichon Frisé may never have lived in the wild, but he is born with the survival skills and the mentality of a meat-eating predator who hunts in a pack. A wolf living in a pack owes its existence to mutual co-operation and an acceptance of a hierarchy, as this ensures both food and protection. A domesticated dog living in a family pack has exactly the same outlook. He wants food, companionship, and leadership – and it is your job to provide for these needs.

YOUR ROLE

Theories about dog behaviour and methods of training go in and out of fashion, but in reality, nothing has changed from the

Do you have what it takes to be a firm, fair and consistent leader?

happy to see someone else shoulder the responsibility. Problems will arise only if you cut a poor figure as leader and the dog feels he should mount a challenge for the top-ranking role.

HOW TO BE A GOOD LEADER

There are a number of guidelines to follow to establish yourself in the role of leader in a way that your Bichon understands and respects. If you have a puppy, you may think you don't have to take this on board for a few months, but that would be a big mistake. Start as you mean to go on, and your pup will be quick to find his place in his new family.

- **Keep it simple:** Decide on the rules you want your Bichon to obey and always make it 100 per cent clear what is acceptable, and what is unacceptable, behaviour.
- **Be consistent:** If you are not consistent about enforcing rules, how can you expect your Bichon to take you seriously? There is nothing worse than allowing your Bichon to jump up on the sofa one moment and then scolding him the next time he does it because he is muddy. As far as the Bichon is concerned, he may as well try it on because he can't predict your reaction.
- **Get your timing right:** If you are rewarding your Bichon, and equally if you are reprimanding him, you must respond within one to two seconds, otherwise the dog will not link his behaviour with your reaction.

day when wolves ventured in from the wild to join the family circle. The wolf (and equally the dog) accepts a subservient place in the family pack in return for food and protection. In a dog's eyes, you are his leader, and he relies on you to make all the important decisions. This does not mean that you have to act like a dictator or a bully. You are accepted as a leader, without argument, as long as you have the right credentials.

The first part of the job is easy.

You are the provider, and you are therefore respected because you supply food. In a Bichon's eyes, you must be the ultimate hunter because a day never goes by when you cannot find food. The second part of the leader's job description is straightforward, but for some reason we find it hard to achieve. In order for a dog to accept his place in the family pack he must respect his leader as the decision-maker. A low-ranking pack animal does not question authority; he is perfectly

82

- **Read your dog's body language:** Find out how to read body language and facial expressions (see below) so that you understand your Bichon's feelings and his intentions.
- **Be aware of your own body language:** A dog will read your body language, and will react on what he sees. If you are calm and quiet around your Bichon, he will pick up on these vibes, and respect your unspoken authority. You can also help your dog to learn by using your body language to communicate with him. For example, if you want your Bichon to come to you, open out your arms and look inviting. If you want your dog to stay, use a hand signal (palm flat, facing the dog) so you are effectively 'blocking' his advance.
- **Tone of voice:** Dogs are very receptive to tone of voice – and you will find that a Bichon is especially responsive. You can use your voice to praise him or to correct undesirable behaviour. If you are pleased with your Bichon, praise him to the skies in a warm, happy voice. If you want to stop him running off with a forbidden 'treasure', use a deep, stern voice when you say "No".
- **Give one command only:** If you keep repeating a command, or keep changing it, your Bichon will think you are babbling and will probably ignore you. If your Bichon does

Be consistent so your Bichon understands what you want him to do.

not respond the first time you ask, make it simple by using a treat to lure him into position, and then you can reward him for a correct response.

- **Daily reminders:** A young, lively Bichon is apt to forget his manners from time to time, and an adolescent dog may try his luck (see page 96). Rather than coming down on your Bichon like a ton of bricks when he does something wrong, try to prevent bad manners by daily reminders of good manners. For example:
  i. Do not let your dog barge ahead of you when you are going through a door.
  ii Do not let him leap out of the car the moment you open the door (which could be potentially lethal, as well as being disrespectful).
  iii. Do not let him eat from your hand when you are at the table.
  iv. Do not let him 'win' a toy at the end of a play session and then make off with it. You 'own' his toys, and you must end every play session on your terms.

UNDERSTANDING YOUR BICHON FRISÉ
Body language is an important means of communication between dogs, which they use to make friends, to assert status, and to avoid conflict. It is important to get on your dog's wavelength by understanding his body language and reading his facial expressions.

- A positive body posture and a wagging tail indicate a happy, confident dog.
- A crouched body posture with ears back and tail down show that a dog is being submissive. A dog may do this when he is being told off or if a more

If you watch dogs meeting and greeting, you will start to understand their body language.

assertive dog approaches him.

- A bold dog will stand tall, looking strong and alert. His ears will be forward and his tail will be held high.

- A playful dog will go down on his front legs while standing on his hind legs in a bow position. This friendly invitation says: "I'm no threat, let's play."

- A dominant, aggressive dog will meet other dogs with a hard stare. If he is challenged, he may bare his teeth and growl, and the corners of his mouth will be drawn forward. His ears will be forward and he will appear tense in every muscle.

- A nervous dog will often show aggressive behaviour as a means of self-protection. If threatened, this dog will lower

his head and flatten his ears. The corners of his mouth may be drawn back, and he may bark or whine.

- Some dogs are 'smilers', curling up their top lip and showing their teeth when they greet people. This should never be confused with a snarl, which would be accompanied by the upright posture of a dominant dog. A smiling dog will have a low body posture and a wagging tail; he is being submissive and it is a greeting that is often used when low-ranking animals greet high-ranking animals in a pack.

GIVING REWARDS

Why should your Bichon do as you ask? If you follow the guidelines given above, your Bichon should respect your

authority, but what about the time when he is playing with a new doggy friend or has found a really enticing scent? The answer is that you must always be the most interesting, the most attractive, and the most irresistible person in your Bichon's eyes. It would be nice to think you could achieve this by personality alone, but most of us need a little extra help. You need to find out what is the biggest reward for your dog. In a Bichon's case, it will often be food, so give him a treat when he does as you ask. For some Bichons, the reward might be a play with a favourite toy but, whatever it is, it must be something that your dog really wants. This can be tricky with a Bichon, who is so interested in the world about him that he is

GIVING REWARDS

Some Bichons see a game as a bigger reward than being given food treats.

This Bichon considers a lick of cheese to be a high value reward.

not always prepared to focus on either a food treat or a toy, but the secret is to persevere until your Bichon starts to value the reward you are offering.

When you are teaching a dog a new exercise, you should reward him frequently. When he knows the exercise or command, reward him randomly so that he keeps on responding to you in a positive manner. If your dog does something extra special, like giving up a stolen 'treasure' the first time you ask, make sure he really knows how pleased you are by giving him a handful of treats

or having a really good game with his favourite toy. If he gets a bonanza reward, he is more likely to co-operate on future occasions, because you have proved to be even more rewarding than his previous activity.

TOP TREATS

Some trainers grade treats depending on what they are asking the dog to do – and this works well for Bichons. Give your Bichon a low-grade treat, such as a piece of dry food, to reward good behaviour on a

random basis, such as sitting when you open a door or allowing you to examine his teeth. But high-grade treats, such as sausage or chicken, are reserved for training new exercises or for use in the park when you want a really good recall. Whatever type of treat you use, remember to subtract it from your Bichon's daily ration. Fat Bichons are lethargic, prone to health problems, and will almost certainly have a shorter life expectancy. Reward your Bichon, but always keep a check on his figure!

THE CLICKER REVOLUTION

Karen Pryor pioneered the technique of clicker training when she was working with dolphins. Karen wanted to mark 'correct' behaviour at the precise moment it happened. She found it was impossible to toss a fish to a dolphin when it was in mid-air, when she wanted to reward it. Her aim was to establish a conditioned response so the dolphin knew that it had performed correctly and a reward would follow.

The solution was the clicker: a small matchbox-shaped training aid, with a metal tongue that makes a click when it is pressed. To begin with, the dolphin had to learn that a click meant that food was coming. The dolphin then learnt that it must 'earn' a click in order to get a reward. Clicker training has been used with many different animals, most particularly with dogs, and it has proved hugely successful. It is a great aid for pet owners and is also widely used by professional trainers who are training highly specialised skills.

HOW DO DOGS LEARN?

It is not difficult to get inside your Bichon's head and understand how he learns, as it is not dissimilar to the way we learn. Dogs learn by conditioning: they find out that specific behaviours produce specific consequences. This is known as operant conditioning or consequence learning. Consequences have to be immediate or clearly linked to the behaviour, as a dog sees the world in terms of action and result. Dogs will quickly learn if an action has a bad consequence or a good consequence.

Dogs also learn by association.

This is known as classical conditioning or association learning. It is the type of learning made famous by Pavlov's experiment with dogs. Pavlov presented dogs with food and measured their salivary response (how much they drooled). Then he rang a bell just before presenting the food. At first, the dogs did not salivate until the food was presented. But after a while they learnt that the sound of the bell meant that food was coming, and so they salivated when they heard the bell. A dog needs to learn the association in order for it to have any meaning. For example, a dog that has never

seen a lead before will be completely indifferent to it. A dog that has learnt that a lead means he is going for a walk will get excited the second he sees the lead; he has learnt to associate a lead with a walk.

BE POSITIVE

The most effective method of training dogs is to use their ability to learn by consequence and to teach that the behaviour you want produces a good consequence. For example, if you ask your Bichon to "Sit", and reward him with a treat, he will learn that it is worth his while to sit on command because it will lead to a treat. He is far more likely to repeat the behaviour, and the behaviour will become stronger, because it results in a positive outcome. This method of training is known as positive reinforcement, and it generally leads to a happy, co-operative dog that is willing to work, and a handler who has fun training their dog.

The opposite approach is negative reinforcement. This is far less effective and often results in a poor relationship between dog and owner. In this method of training, you ask your Bichon to "Sit", and, if he does not respond, you deliver a sharp yank on the training collar or push his rear to the ground. The dog learns that not responding to your command has a bad consequence, and he may be less likely to ignore you in the future. However, it may well have a bad consequence for you, too. A dog that is treated in this way may associate harsh handling with the handler and become aggressive or fearful. Instead of establishing a pattern of willing co-operation, you are establishing a relationship built on coercion.

GETTING STARTED

As you train your Bichon, you will develop your own techniques as you get to know what motivates him. You may decide to get involved with clicker training or you may prefer to go for a simple command-and-reward formula. It does not matter what form of training you use, as long as it is based on positive, reward-based methods.

There are a few important guidelines to bear in mind when you are training your Bichon:

• Start training from an early age. The Bichon may be small in stature, but he is big on personality and needs to be trained just as much as a larger dog.

A Bichon will quickly become bored if training is dull and repetitious.

- Find a training area that is free from distractions, particularly when you are just starting out.
- Keep training sessions short, especially with young puppies that have very short attention spans.
- A Bichon will quickly become bored if you attempt to drill him, or become too repetitive when you are training exercises. Break up training sessions with games, and keep changing what you are doing so your Bichon is kept on his toes!
- Do not train if you are in a bad mood or if you are on a tight schedule – the training session will be doomed to failure.
- If you are using a toy as a reward, make sure it is only available when you are training. In this way it has an added value for your Bichon. Remember, a Bichon is very clever at finding goodies, so keep his toy well out of reach.
- If you are using food treats, make sure they are bite-size and easy to swallow; you don't want to hang about while your Bichon chews on his treat.
- All food treats must be deducted from your Bichon's daily food ration.
- When you are training, move around your allocated area so that your dog does not think that an exercise can only be performed in one place.

It will not take your Bichon long to learn that he must 'earn' a click before he gets a reward.

- If your Bichon is finding an exercise difficult, try not to get frustrated. Go back a step and praise him for his effort. You will probably find he is more successful when you try again at the next training session.
- Always end training sessions on a happy, positive note. Ask your Bichon to do something you know he can do – it could be a trick he enjoys performing, such as standing on his hind legs, which comes naturally to all Bichons, and then reward him with a few treats or an extra-long play session.
- Most important of all – make training sessions fun!

In the exercises that follow,

clicker training is introduced and followed, but all the exercises will work without the use of a clicker.

INTRODUCING A CLICKER

This is very easy, and a Bichon who loves his food will learn about the clicker in record time. It can be combined with attention training, which is a very useful tool and can be used on many different occasions.

- Prepare some treats and go to an area that is free from distractions. When your Bichon stops sniffing around and looks at you, click and reward by throwing him a treat. This means he will not crowd you, but will go looking for the treat. Repeat a couple of times. If your Bichon is very easily distracted, you may need to start this exercise with the dog on a lead.
- After a few clicks, your Bichon will understand that if he hears a click, he will get a treat. He must now learn that he must 'earn' a click. This time, when your Bichon looks at you, wait a little longer before clicking, and then reward him. If your Bichon is on a lead but responding well, try him off the lead.
- When your Bichon is working

for a click and giving you his attention, you can introduce a cue or command word, such as "Watch". Repeat a few times, using the cue. You now have a Bichon that understands the clicker and will give you his attention when you ask him to "Watch".

TRAINING EXERCISES

THE SIT
This is the easiest exercise to teach, so it is rewarding for both you and your Bichon.
- Choose a tasty treat and hold it just above your puppy's nose. As he looks up at the treat, he will naturally go into the Sit. As soon as he is in position, reward him.
- Repeat the exercise, and when your pup understands what you want, introduce the "Sit" command
- You can practice at mealtimes by holding out the bowl and waiting for your dog to sit. Most Bichons learn this one very quickly!

THE DOWN
Work hard at this exercise because a reliable Down is useful in many different situations, and an instant Down can be a lifesaver.
- You can start with your dog in a Sit, or it is just as effective to teach it when the dog is standing. Hold a treat just below your puppy's nose and slowly lower it towards the ground. The treat acts as a lure, and your puppy will

This Bichon has learnt a swift response to the "Down".

follow it, first going down on his forequarters, and then bringing his hindquarters down as he tries to get the treat.
- Make sure you close your fist around the treat, and only reward your puppy with the treat when he is in the correct position. If your puppy is reluctant to go Down, you can apply gentle pressure on his shoulders to encourage him to go into the correct position.
- When your puppy is following the treat and going into position, introduce a verbal command.
- Build up this exercise over a period of time, each time

waiting a little longer before giving the reward, so the puppy learns to stay in the Down position.

THE RECALL
This is a companionable breed and, in general, a Bichon will prefer not to stray too far from his owner when he is out on a walk. But this cannot be relied upon. The Bichon has 'dizzy' moments when he will take off at the speed of light, and then seem to have no recollection of which direction he came from. This is not a scenting breed, so a lost Bichon has little chance of tracking his way back to his owner.

COMING WHEN CALLED

There are times when your Bichon gets distracted, and may become 'deaf' to your calls.

When you get your Bichon's attention, make yourself sound exciting so that he wants to come to you.

For this reason, it is vital to build up a strong response to the Recall. But also exercise great caution when you let your Bichon off lead, checking the environment to make sure he cannot stray too far from you. For example, an enclosed playing field would be a safe option; open moorland would not.

There is another reason why you should evaluate the environment before allowing your Bichon off lead. In a busy park there may be other, larger dogs running loose. The Bichon is not a common breed, and another dog could well mistake your pet dog for a large, white rabbit. Natural instincts to chase or kill can take over with dire consequences.

- If you have a puppy it is best to start Recall training almost from the moment he arrives home, as he will instinctively want to follow you. Make sure you are always happy and excited when your Bichon comes to you, even if he has been slower than you would like.

- Practise in the garden, and, when your puppy is busy exploring, get his attention by calling his name. As he runs towards you, introduce the command "Come". Make sure you sound happy and exciting, so your puppy wants to come to you. When he responds, give him lots of praise and reward him with a tasty treat.

- If your puppy is slow to respond, try running away a few paces, or jumping up and down. It doesn't matter how silly you look, the key issue is to get your puppy's attention, and then make yourself irresistible!

- In a dog's mind, coming when called should be regarded as the best fun because he knows he is always going to be rewarded. Never make the mistake of telling your dog off, no matter how slow he is to respond, as you will undo all your previous hard work.

- When you are free running your dog, make sure you have his favourite toy, or a pocket full of treats, so you can reward

90

SECRET WEAPON

You can build up a strong Recall by using another form of association learning. Buy a whistle, and when you are giving your Bichon his food, peep on the whistle. You can choose the type of signal you want to give: two short peeps, or one long whistle, for example. Within a matter of days, your dog will learn that the sound of the whistle means food is coming.

Now transfer the lesson outside. Arm yourself with some tasty treats and the whistle. Allow your Bichon to run free in the garden, and, after a couple of minutes, use the whistle. The dog has already learnt to associate the whistle with food, so he will come towards you. Immediately reward him with a treat and lots of praise.

Repeat the lesson a few times in the garden so you are confident that your dog is responding before trying it in the park. Make sure you always have some treats in your pocket when you go for a walk, and your dog will quickly learn how rewarding it is to come to you.

him at intervals throughout the walk when you call him to you. Do not allow your dog to free run and only call him back at the end of the walk to clip his lead on. An intelligent Bichon will soon realise that the Recall means the end of his walk, and the end of fun – so who can blame him for not wanting to come back?

• The biggest mistake is to let your Bichon off-lead before he has a reliable response to the Recall. If your dog gets into the habit of ignoring you or running off, you will find it very difficult to retrain him. The best plan is to practise in the garden, always rewarding your Bichon when he comes to

you. Then, when he is about six months old, you can try free-running him, as by this time, he will have built up a strong response to the Recall, and it will not occur to him to ignore you.

TRAINING LINE
This is the equivalent of a very long lead, which you can buy at a pet store, or you can make your own with a length of rope. The training line is attached to your Bichon's collar and should be around 15 feet (4.5 metres) in length.

The purpose of the training line is to prevent your Bichon from disobeying you so that he never has the chance to get into bad

habits. For example, when you call your Bichon and he ignores you, you can immediately pick up the end of the training line and call him again. By picking up the line you will have attracted his attention, and if you call in an excited, happy voice, your Bichon will come to you. The moment he comes to you, give him a tasty treat so he is instantly rewarded for making the 'right' decision.

WALKING ON A LOOSE LEAD
This is a simple exercise, which baffles many Bichon owners. In most cases, owners delay training until their Bichon has become an unruly youngster, or they are too impatient, wanting to get on with the expedition

rather than training the dog to walk on a lead. Take time with this one; a Bichon that pulls or drags on the lead is no pleasure to own.

- Make lead training fun. Start by going in the garden, and simply having a game with the lead so that your Bichon builds up a good association with it.
- In the early stages of lead training, attach the lead to the collar, allow your puppy to pick his route and follow him. He will get used to the feeling of being 'attached' to you and has no reason to put up any resistance. Let him walk for a few paces, and then have a game.
- Next, find a toy or a tasty treat and show it to your puppy. Let him follow the treat/toy for a few paces, and then reward him or have a game.
- Build up the amount of time your pup will walk with you, and when he is walking nicely by your side, introduce the verbal command "Heel" or "Close". Give lots of praise when your pup is in the correct position.
- When your pup is walking alongside you, keep focusing his attention on you by using his name, and then rewarding him when he looks at you. If it is going well, introduce some changes of direction.

A well trained Bichon will walk on a loose lead, giving attention when requested.

- Do not attempt to take your puppy out on the lead until you have mastered the basics at home. You need to be confident that your puppy accepts the lead and will focus his attention on you, when requested, before you face the challenge of a busy environment.
- As your Bichon becomes more confident, he may try to pull on the lead, particularly if you are heading somewhere he wants to go, such as the park. If this happens, stop, call your dog to you, and do not set off again until he is in the correct position. It may take time, but your Bichon will eventually realise that it is more

productive to walk by your side than to pull ahead.

The key is to make your Bichon believe that lead training is all part of a game. Keep the mood light-hearted and positive, and you will soon have a dog that trots along happily beside you.

STAYS

This may not be the most exciting exercise, but it is one of the most useful. There are many occasions when you want your Bichon to stay in position, even if it is only for a few seconds. The classic example is when you want your Bichon to stay in the back of the car until you have clipped on his lead. Some trainers use the verbal command "Stay" when the dog is to stay in position for an extended period of time, and "Wait" if the dog is to stay in position for a few seconds until you give the next command. Others trainers use a universal "Stay" to cover all situations. It all comes down to personal preference, and, as long as you are consistent, your dog will understand the command he is given.

- Put your puppy in a Sit or a Down, and use a hand signal (flat palm, facing the dog) to show he is to stay in position. Step a pace away from the dog. Wait a second, step back and

Your Bichon may feel more secure if you teach him to "Stay" when he is in the Down position.

reward him. If you have a lively pup, you may find it easier to train this exercise on the lead.

- Repeat the exercise, gradually increasing the distance you can leave your dog. When you return to your dog's side, praise him quietly, and release him with a command, such as "OK".

- Remember to keep you body language very still when you are training this exercise, and avoid eye contact with your dog. Work on this exercise over a period of time, and you will build up a really reliable Stay.

SOCIALISATION

While your Bichon is mastering basic obedience exercises, there is other, equally important, work to do with him. A Bichon is not only becoming a part of your home and family, he is becoming a member of the community. He needs to be able to live in the outside world, coping calmly with every new situation that comes his way. It is your job to introduce him to as many different experiences as possible, and encourage him to behave in an appropriate manner.

In order to socialise your

Bichon effectively, it is helpful to understand how his brain is developing, and then you will get a perspective on how he sees the world.

CANINE SOCIALISATION
(Birth to 7 weeks)
This is the time when a dog learns how to be a dog. By interacting with his mother and his littermates, a young pup learns about leadership and submission. He learns to read body posture so that he understands the intentions of his mother and his siblings. A

Young puppies learn vital lessons when they are interacting with their siblings.

puppy that is taken away from his litter too early may always have behavioural problems with other dogs, either being fearful or aggressive.

SOCIALISATION PERIOD (7 to 12 weeks)

This is the time to get cracking and introduce your Bichon puppy to as many different experiences as possible. This includes meeting different people, other dogs and animals, seeing new sights, and hearing a range of sounds – from the vacuum cleaner to the roar of traffic. At this stage, a puppy learns very quickly and what he learns will stay with him for the rest of his life. This is the best time for a puppy to move to a new home, as he is adaptable and ready to form deep bonds.

FEAR-IMPRINT PERIOD (8 to 11 weeks)

This occurs during the socialisation period, and it can be the cause of problems if it is not handled carefully. If a pup is exposed to a frightening or painful experience, it will lead to lasting impressions. Obviously, you will attempt to avoid frightening situations, such as your pup being bullied by a mean-spirited older dog, or a firework going off, but you cannot always protect your puppy from the unexpected. If your pup has a nasty experience, the best plan is to make light of it and distract him by offering him a treat or a game. The pup will take the lead from you and will be reassured that there is nothing to worry about. If you mollycoddle him and sympathise with him, he is far more likely to retain the memory of his fear.

SENIORITY PERIOD (12 to 16 weeks)

During this period, your Bichon puppy starts to cut the apron strings and becomes more independent. He will test out his status to find out who is the pack leader: him or you. Bad habits, such as play-biting, which may have been seen as endearing a few weeks earlier, should be firmly discouraged. Remember to use positive, reward-based training, but make sure your puppy knows that you are the leader and must be respected.

SECOND FEAR-IMPRINT PERIOD (6 to 14 months)

This period is not as critical as the first fear-imprint period, but it should still be handled carefully. During this time your Bichon may appear apprehensive, or he may show fear of something familiar.

A dog that is well socialised will take all situations in his stride.

You may feel as if you have taken a backwards step, but if you adopt a calm, positive manner, your Bichon will see that there is nothing to be frightened of. Do not make your dog confront the thing that frightens him. Simply distract his attention, and give him something else to think about, such as obeying a simple command, such as "Sit" or "Down". This will give you the opportunity to praise and reward your dog, and will help to boost his confidence.

YOUNG ADULTHOOD AND MATURITY (1 to 4 years)

The timing of this phase depends on the size of the dog: the bigger the dog, the later it is. This period coincides with a dog's increasing maturity, mental as well as physical. Some dogs, particularly those with an assertive nature, will test your leadership again and may become aggressive towards other dogs. Firmness and continued training are essential at this time so that your Bichon accepts his status in the family pack.

IDEAS FOR SOCIALISATION

When you are socialising your Bichon, you want him to experience as many different situations as possible. Try out some of the following ideas, which will ensure he has an allround education.

If you are taking on a rescued dog and have little knowledge of his background, it is important to work through a programme of socialisation. A young puppy soaks up new experiences like a sponge, but an older dog can still learn. If a rescued dog shows fear or apprehension, treat him in exactly the same way as you would treat a youngster who is going through the second fearimprint period.

- Accustom your puppy to household noises, such as the vacuum cleaner, the television and the washing machine.
- Ask visitors to come to the door, wearing different types of clothing – for example, wearing a hat, a long raincoat, or carrying a stick or an umbrella.
- If you do not have children at home, make sure your Bichon has a chance to meet and play with them. Go to a local park and watch children in the play area. You will not be able to take your Bichon inside the play area, but he will see children playing and will get used to their shouts of excitement.

TRAINING CLUBS

There are lots of training clubs to choose from. Your vet will probably have details of clubs in your area, or you can ask friends who have dogs if they attend a club. Alternatively, use the internet to find out more information. But how do you know if the club is any good?

Before you take your dog, ask if you can go to a class as an observer and find out the following:
• What experience does the instructor(s) have?
• Do they have experience with Bichon Frisé?
• Is the class well organised and are the dogs reasonably quiet? (A noisy class indicates a

unruly atmosphere, which will not be conducive to learning.)
• Are there are a number of classes to suit dogs of different ages and abilities?
• Are positive, reward-based training methods used?
• Does the club train for the Good Citizen Scheme (see page 109)?

If you are not happy with the training club, find another one. An inexperienced instructor who cannot handle a number of dogs in a confined environment can do more harm than good.

• Attend puppy classes. These are designed for puppies between the ages of 12 to 20 weeks, and give them a chance to play and interact together in a controlled, supervised environment. Your vet will have details of a local class.
• Take a walk around some quiet streets, such as a residential area, so your Bichon can get used to the sound of traffic. As he becomes more confident, progress to busier areas.
• Go to a railway station. You don't have to get on a train if you don't need to, but your Bichon will have the chance to experience trains – people wheeling luggage, loudspeaker

announcements, and going up and down stairs and over railway bridges.
• If you live in the town, plan a trip to the country. You can enjoy a day out and provide an opportunity for your Bichon to see livestock, such as sheep, cattle and horses.
• One of the best places for socialising a dog is at a country fair. There will be crowds of people, livestock in pens, tractors, bouncy castles, fairground rides and food stalls.
• When your dog is over 20 weeks of age, find a training class for adult dogs. Your local training class may have both puppy and adult classes.

THE ADOLESCENT BICHON

It happens to every dog – and every owner. One minute you have an obedient well-behaved youngster, and the next you have an adolescent who appears to have forgotten everything he learnt. This applies equally to males and females, although the type of adolescent behaviour, and its onset, varies between individuals.

In most cases a Bichon male will hit adolescence at around 8 to 10 months, although some lines are slower to mature. It has been noted that some American-bred Bichons mature more slowly, both mentally and physically. In most cases, a male Bichon will not change dramatically in personality at this

It is not unusual for a Bichon to go through some behavioural changes during adolescence.

time, particularly in relation to people. However, he may pay more attention to bitches, and he may attempt to be more assertive with other male dogs. It is very much a time when the adolescent male is feeling his feet and finding his place in the adult dog world.

Female Bichons are quicker to mature than males. The significant physical change comes with their first season, which is usually at around seven to eight months. Some females may become a little introspective at this time, but the majority carry on pretty much as normal.

An adolescent Toy dog may not go through such dramatic behavioural changes as some of the larger breeds, but it can be a trying time in a dog's life, and it can be slightly stressful to have a dog who is acting out of character. However, it is important to remember that it is only a passing phase on the journey to becoming a fully fledged adult.

WHEN THINGS GO WRONG
Positive, reward-based training has proved to be the most effective method of teaching dogs, but what happens when your Bichon does something wrong and you need to show him that his behaviour is

As a dog matures, he may start to test your leadership.

unacceptable? The old-fashioned school of dog training used to rely on the powers of punishment and negative reinforcement. A dog who raided the bin, for example, was smacked. Now we have learnt that it is not only unpleasant and cruel to hit a dog, it is also ineffective. If you hit a dog for stealing, he is more than likely to see *you* as the bad consequence of stealing, so he may raid the bin again, but probably not when you are around. If he raided the bin some time before you discovered it, he will be even more confused by your punishment, as he will not relate your response to his 'crime'.

A more commonplace example is when a dog fails to respond to a recall in the park. When the dog eventually comes back, the owner puts the dog on the lead and goes straight home to punish the dog for his poor response. Unfortunately, the dog will have a different interpretation. He does not think: "I won't ignore a recall command because the bad consequence is the end of my play in the park." He thinks: "Coming to my owner resulted in the end of playtime – therefore coming to my owner has a bad consequence so I won't do that again."

There are a number of strategies to tackle undesirable behaviour – and they have nothing to do with harsh handling.

Ignoring bad behaviour: A lot of undesirable behaviour in Bichons comes down to attention seeking. A Bichon believes that he should be loved and adored – and this is part of his charm. However, he must learn that he cannot have attention on demand, because this is not always possible. There are times when you are too busy to drop everything because your Bichon wants a cuddle, or if you have another dog, you may want to give him some attention. Remember, the Bichon is an intelligent dog, and he can also be very manipulative. If a Bichon gets away with barking at you in order to get your attention, he will continue doing it. In no time, this will become habit forming – and you will find it very hard to retrain him.

The key is to get in early so that your Bichon learns that his attention-seeking strategies are not working. For example, if your Bichon likes the sound of his own voice, do not react by shouting at him, telling him to be "quiet". As far as a Bichon is concerned, he has got what he wanted – your attention. You are joining in a 'conversation' with him, regardless of how loud you are shouting. So, if your Bichon starts barking, ignore him. Avoid eye contact and turn your back on him. The moment he is quiet, you can call him to you and give lots of praise, and maybe a treat. You can also focus his attention by having a game with a toy, or doing a simple training exercise. If a Bichon is engaged with you, he will have no need to bark as he has got your attention.

You may have to work on this over a period of time, but a Bichon picks things up easily and will only repeat the behaviour that works for him. It will not take him long to realise that barking gets no response, whereas being quiet earns him a bonanza reward. Being ignored is a worst-case scenario for a Bichon, so remember to use it as an effective training tool.

Stopping bad behaviour: There are occasions when you want to call an instant halt to whatever it is your Bichon is doing. He may have run off with something that he should not have, or you may have caught him red-handed in the rubbish bin. He has already committed the 'crime', so your aim is to stop him and to redirect his attention. You can do this by using a deep, firm tone of voice to say "No", which will startle him, and then call him to you in a bright, happy voice. If necessary, you can attract him with a toy or a treat. The moment your Bichon stops the undesirable behaviour and comes towards you, reward his good behaviour. You can back this up by running through a couple of simple exercises, such as a Sit or a Down, and rewarding with treats. In this way, your Bichon focuses his attention on you, and sees you as the greatest source of reward and pleasure.

In a more extreme situation, when you want to interrupt undesirable behaviour and you know that a simple "No" will not do the trick, you can try

There are times when you catch your Bichon red-handed and you need to call an instant halt to his behaviour.

something a little more dramatic. If you get a can and fill it with pebbles, it will make a really loud noise when you shake it or throw it. The same effect can be achieved with purpose-made training discs. The dog will be startled and stop what he is doing. Even better, the dog will not associate the unpleasant noise with you. This gives you the perfect opportunity to be the nice guy, calling the dog to you and giving him lots of praise.

PROBLEM BEHAVIOUR
If you have trained your Bichon from puppyhood and established yourself as a fair and consistent leader, you will end up with a brilliant companion dog. The Bichon is a loving and affectionate dog who is eager to please and rarely has hang-ups. For most Bichons, the key to contentment is spending time with their owners.

However, problems may arise unexpectedly, or you may have taken on a rescued Bichon that has behavioural problems. If you are worried about your Bichon and feel out of your depth, do not delay in seeking professional help. This is readily available, usually through a referral from your vet, or you can find out additional information on the internet (see Appendices for web addresses). An animal behaviourist will have experience in tackling problem behaviour and will be able to help both you and your dog.

It is natural for puppies to grab hold of each other when they are playing together.

MOUTHING

Puppies explore the world with their mouths and with their noses. They pick up different scents, and if they come across something new, they will investigate using their mouth and teeth. Littermates will play together, mouthing and biting each other, and they will often play with their mother in the same way. Crucially, a puppy learns to stop biting if his mother or a littermate let out a shriek of pain, or growl a warning.

When a puppy arrives in his new home, he will still want to explore by mouthing. It is your job to show him that, right from the start, that mouthing, nibbling or nipping people is unacceptable. It is vitally important to do this from day one so your puppy does not learn to assert his will by biting. This is particularly important with a breed that needs constant grooming. Most Bichons love being groomed, but a puppy who has not had sufficient handling, may resent the attention and try to evade it by mouthing at your hand as you attempt to groom him. This is not typical Bichon behaviour; it is the consequence of a poor upbringing.

The best way of inhibiting mouthing or nipping is to copy what the puppy has already learnt in the nest while he was growing up with his siblings:

- If your Bichon tries to mouth or nip, give a sharp cry so he realises he has stepped out of line.
- Then offer him a treat in the palm of your hand, and ask

him to take it "Gently".
- Keep repeating this exercise so your Bichon learns that it is more rewarding to stop mouthing. He will see that a hand is offering him a treat rather than seeing it as fingers to nibble.
- If you have children, supervise all interactions to make sure your Bichon is not getting over-excited and resorting to mouthing.

If you have taken on a rescued dog that has mouthing or nipping problems, you may need to seek professional advice.

SEPARATION ANXIETY

The Bichon loves his human family and will become very unhappy and anxious if he is left alone for long periods. This is particularly true if you have a single Bichon who cannot fall back on canine company in your absence. However, regardless of whether you have a single Bichon or a pack, every dog should be able to tolerate some time on his own without becoming stressed.

A new puppy should be left for short periods on his own, ideally in a crate where he cannot get up to any mischief. It is a good idea to leave him with a boredom-busting toy, such as a kong filled with food, so he will be happily occupied in your absence. When you return, do not rush to the crate and make a huge fuss. Wait a few minutes, and then calmly go to the crate and release your dog, telling him how good he has been. If this scenario is repeated a number of times, your Bichon will soon learn that being left on his own is no big deal.

Problems with separation anxiety are most likely to arise if you take on a rescued dog who has major insecurities. You may also find your Bichon hates being left if you have failed to accustom him to short periods of isolation when he was growing up. Separation anxiety is expressed in a number of ways, and all are equally distressing for both dog and owner. An anxious dog who is left alone may bark and whine continuously, urinate and defecate, and may be extremely destructive.
There are a number of steps you can take when attempting to solve this problem.

- Put up a baby-gate between adjoining rooms, and leave your dog in one room while you are in the other room. Your dog will be able to see you and hear you, but he is learning to cope without being right next to you. Build up the amount of time you can leave your dog in easy stages.
- Buy some boredom-busting toys and fill them with some tasty treats. Whenever you leave your dog, give him a food-filled toy so that he is busy while you are away.
- If you have not used a crate before, it is not too late to start. Make sure the crate is cosy and 'den-like', and train your Bichon to get used to going inside while you are in the same room. Gradually build up the amount of time he spends in the crate, and then start leaving the room for short periods. When you return, do not make a fuss of your dog. Leave him for five or 10 minutes before releasing him so that he gets used to your comings and goings.
- Pretend to go out, putting on your coat and jangling keys, but do not leave the house. An anxious dog often becomes hyped up by the ritual of leavetaking, so this will help to desensitise him.
- When you go out, leave a radio or a TV on. Some dogs are comforted by hearing voices and background noise when they are left alone.
- Try to make your absences as short as possible when you are

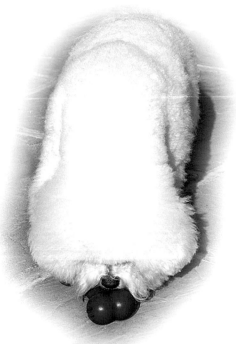

Provide a boredom busting toy, such as a Kong filled with food, which will give your Bichon something to occupy himself with in your absence.

first training your dog to accept being on his own. When you return, do not fuss your dog, rushing to his crate to release him. Leave him for a few minutes, and when you go to him remain calm and relaxed so that he does not become hyped up with a huge greeting.

If you take these steps, your dog should become less anxious, and, over a period of time, you should be able to solve the problem. However, if you are failing to make progress, do not delay in calling in expert help.

RESOURCE GUARDING

Sometimes a Bichon will 'adopt' a toy and be reluctant to give it up.

If your Bichon is trying to guard his food bowl, drop in some extra treats so that he welcomes your intervention.

RESOURCE GUARDING

The Bichon is rarely assertive in his behaviour, but he is a clever dog who is capable of manipulating situations to his advantage. In some cases, a Bichon may find something he wants, and then become possessive in order to guard what he sees as a valuable resource. This may take a number of different forms:

• A Bichon may become possessive over his food bowl and growl if you approach him when he is eating.
• He may adopt a favourite toy and refuse to give it up when requested.
• He may decide the sofa is the best place to lie and growl a warning if you ask him to move.

If you see signs of your Bichon becoming manipulative, you must work at lowering his status so that he realises that you are the leader and he does not have the right to guard resources. Although you need to be firm, you also need to use positive training methods so that your Bichon is rewarded for the behaviour you want. In this way, his 'correct' behaviour will be strengthened and repeated.

There are a number of steps you can take to teach your Bichon that you are in control. They include:

• Go back to basics and hold daily training sessions. Make

AGGRESSION

Aggression is a complex issue, as there are different causes and the behaviour may be triggered by numerous factors. It may be directed towards people, but far more commonly it is directed towards other dogs. Aggression in dogs may be the result of:

• Assertive behaviour (see also page 81).
• Defensive behaviour: This may be induced by fear, pain or punishment.
• Territory. A dog may become aggressive if strange dogs or people enter his territory (which is generally seen as the house and garden).
• Intra-sexual issues: This is aggression between sexes – male-to-male or female-to-female.
• Parental instinct: A mother dog may become aggressive if she is protecting her puppies.

A dog who has been well socialised (see page 93) and has been given sufficient exposure to other dogs at significant stages of his development will rarely be aggressive. A wellbred Bichon that has been reared correctly should not have a hint of aggression in his temperament. Obviously if you have taken on an older, rescued dog, you will have little or no knowledge of his background, and if he shows signs of aggression, the cause will need to be determined. In most cases, you would be well advised to call in professional help if you see aggressive behaviour in your dog; if the aggression is directed towards people, you should seek immediate advice. This behaviour can escalate very quickly and could lead to disastrous consequences.

sure you have some really tasty treats, or find a toy your Bichon really values and only bring it out at training sessions. Run through some training exercises, and make a big fuss of your Bichon, rewarding him when he does well. This will reinforce the message that you are the leader and that it is rewarding to do as you ask.

• Teach your Bichon something new; this can be as simple as learning a trick, such as begging on command. Having something new to think about will stimulate your Bichon,

and he will benefit from interacting with you.

• If your Bichon is being possessive over his food bowl, put the bowl down empty, and drop in a little food at a time. Periodically stop dropping in the food, and tell your Bichon to "Sit" and "Wait". Wait a few seconds, and then reward him by dropping in more food. He will quickly learn that having you around at mealtimes is a good thing.

• Do not let your Bichon barge through doors ahead of you, or leap from the back of the car before you release him. You

may need to put your dog on the lead and teach him to "Wait" at doorways, and then reward him for letting you go through first.

NEW CHALLENGES

If you enjoy training your Bichon, you may want to try one of the many dog sports that are now on offer.

GOOD CITIZEN SCHEME

This is a scheme run by the Kennel Club in the UK and the American Kennel Club in the USA. The schemes promote responsible ownership and help

The Good Citizen scheme is designed to promote responsible ownership – and dogs that are welcome in the community.

handled by the examiner.
- Stays, with the owner in sight, and then out of sight.
- Food manners, allowing the owner to eat without begging, and taking a treat on command.
- Sendaway – sending the dog to his bed.

The tests are designed to show the control you have over your dog, and his ability to respond correctly and remain calm in all situations. The Good Citizen Scheme is taught at most training clubs. For more information, log on to the Kennel Club or AKC website (see Appendices).

SHOWING

In your eyes, your Bichon is the most beautiful dog in the world – but would a judge agree? Showing is a highly competitive sport, and the Bichon must be correctly presented, which can be very time consuming. However, many owners get bitten by the showing bug, and their calendar is governed by the dates of the top showing fixtures.

To be successful in the show ring, a Bichon must conform as closely as possible to the Breed Standard, which is a written blueprint describing the 'perfect' Bichon Frisé (see Chapter Seven). To get started you need to buy a puppy that has show potential and then train him to perform in the ring. A Bichon will be expected to stand in show pose, gait for the judge in order to show off his natural movement, and be examined by the judge.

you to train a well-behaved dog who will fit in with the community. The schemes are excellent for all pet owners, and they are also a good starting point if you plan to compete with your Bichon when he is older. The KC and the AKC schemes vary in format. In the UK there are three levels: bronze, silver and gold, with each test becoming progressively more demanding. In

the AKC scheme there is a single test.

Some of the exercises include:
- Walking on a loose lead among people and other dogs.
- Recall amid distractions.
- A controlled greeting where dogs stay under control while owners meet.
- The dog allows all-over grooming and handling by his owner, and also accepts being

This involves a detailed hands-on examination, so your Bichon must be bombproof when handled by strangers.

Many training clubs hold ringcraft classes, which are run by experienced showgoers. At these classes, you will learn how to handle your Bichon in the ring, and you will also find out about rules, procedures and show ring etiquette.

The best plan is to start off at some small, informal shows where you can practise and learn the tricks of the trade before graduating to bigger shows. It's a long haul starting in the very first puppy class, but the dream is to make your Bichon up into a Champion.

Showing is highly competitive, but it can be very rewarding if you have a good specimen of the breed.

COMPETITIVE OBEDIENCE

Border Collies and German Shepherds dominate this sport, with gundog breeds making up the numbers. The Bichon is not a natural 'obedience' dog as he is probably too clever. He does not see the point of repetition, and he is more likely to expect *you* to retrieve a dumbbell if you have thrown it! However, in the USA, owners of Toy dogs seem more ready to take on the challenge, and a number of Bichon Frisé have achieved a level of success..

The classes start off being relatively easy and become progressively more complex with additional exercises, and the handler giving minimal instructions to the dog.

Exercises include:

• **Heelwork:** Dog and handler must complete a set pattern on and off the lead, which includes left turns, right turns, about turns, and changes of pace.

• **Recall:** This may be when the handler is stationary or on the move.

• **Retrieve:** This may be a dumbbell or any article chosen by the judge.

• **Sendaway:** The dog is sent to a designated spot and must go into an instant Down until he is recalled by the handler.

• **Stays:** The dog must stay in the Sit and in the Down for a set amount of time. In advanced classes, the handler is out of sight,

• **Scent:** The dog must retrieve a single cloth from a pre-arranged pattern of cloths that has his owner's scent, or, in advanced classes, the judge's scent. There may also be decoy cloths.

• **Distance control.** The dog must execute a series of moves (Sit, Stand, Down) without moving from his position and with the handler at a distance.

Even though competitive obedience requires accuracy and precision, make sure you make it fun for your Bichon, with lots of praise and rewards so that you motivate him to do his best. Many training clubs run advanced classes for those who want to compete in obedience, or you can hire the services of a professional trainer so you can have one-on-one sessions.

The Bichon is more than ready to take on the challenge of agility.

AGILITY

This fun sport has grown enormously in popularity over the past few years, and the active, fast-moving Bichon is more than capable of competing. If you fancy having a go, make sure you have good control over your Bichon and keep him slim. Agility is a very physical sport, which demands fitness from both dog and handler. A fat Bichon is never going to make it as an agility competitor.

In agility competitions, each dog must complete a set course over a series of obstacles, which include:

- Jumps (upright hurdles and long jump)
- Weaves
- A-frame
- Dog walk
- Seesaw
- Tunnels (collapsible and rigid)
- Tyre

Dogs may compete in jumping classes with jumps, tunnels and weaves, or in agility classes, which have the full set of equipment. Faults are given for poles down on the jumps, missed contact points on the A-frame, dog walk and seesaw, as well as refusals. If a dog takes the wrong course, he is eliminated. The winner is the dog that completes the course in the fastest time with no faults. As you progress up the levels, courses become progressively harder with more twists, turns and changes of direction.

If you want to get involved in Agility, you will need to find a club that specialises in the sport (see Appendices). You will not be

The Bichon is an intelligent dog and he will thrive on being given things to do – and earning your praise.

allowed to start training until your Bichon is 12 months old, and you cannot compete until he is 18 months old. This rule is for the protection of the dog, who may suffer injury if he puts strain on bones and joints while he is still growing.

DANCING WITH DOGS

This sport is relatively new, but it is becoming increasingly popular. It is very entertaining to watch, but it is certainly not as simple as it looks. To perform a

choreographed routine to music with your Bichon demands a huge amount of training, but it can be very rewarding.

Dancing with dogs is divided into two categories: Heelwork to Music and Canine Freestyle. In Heelwork to Music the dog must work closely with his handler and show a variety of close 'heelwork' positions. In Canine Freestyle the routine can be more flamboyant, with the dog working at a distance from the handler and performing

spectacular tricks. Routines are judged on style and presentation, content and accuracy.

SUMMING UP

The Bichon Frisé has it all – he is intelligent, full of character, and is a fun and loving companion. Make sure you keep your half of the bargain: spend time socialising and training your Bichon so that you can be proud to take him anywhere and he will always be a credit to you.

THE PERFECT BICHON FRISÉ

Chapter 7

When the Bichon Frisé was first registered with the French Kennel Club, a complete description of every physical and psychological characteristic of the breed was listed by those people who were involved in its initial development. This is known as the Breed Standard, and the breed characteristics described must remain in place, and be easily recognised, if the dog to be considered true to its breed type and therefore a good example of the breed. Responsible and dedicated breeders of the Bichon Frisé will work closely to the Breed Standard in an effort to produce the "perfect" Bichon. In doing so, a Breed Standard will act as a blueprint of the breed. It is a description of an ideal, providing a close step-by-step guideline of each breed characteristic and breed point.

It should also serve to impose restrictions involving points that could, over time, become exaggerated in nature and even detrimental to the overall health of the dog. It may well be an impossible task, as no dog can ever be described as "perfect", but to strive for perfection is the very least any breeder can do if the dogs that are produced are to continue to be typical Bichons and remain as the happy, healthy dogs they are today.

The Breed Standard used in the UK was developed and adapted from the original Federation Cynologique Internnationale (FCI) Standard used by the French breeders when the breed was first recognised back in the 1950s. When the breed was first developed in the United States, American breeders drew up their own Standard. This proved to be even more precise in its description of the breed, but does illustrate a few differences, most significantly concerning the overall size and the presentation of the coat.

However, international competition is now becoming more popular and dogs are being exhibited in the USA, here in the UK, and in Europe with very little difference in type beyond the style of presentation. In the past it was felt that dogs from the Continent brought into the UK were considerably different to those that entered the country from the USA. These dogs were often described as being much bigger and heavier in type, and it was many years after the breed's introduction to the UK before

An English Champion: Ch. Bobander What A Performance, JW ('Vinnie'). Winner of 2 Best In Shows, 15 CCs (7 with Best Of Breed), and 15 Reserve CCs. Bred, owned and handled by Chris Wyatt, Bobander.
Photo: Carol Ann Johnson.

Ch Pamplona Bring Me Sunshine. Top winning Bichon 2009. Grand-son of Ch. & Am. Ch. Parays I Told You So, greatest winning Bichon in the history of the breed in the UK. Owned by Michael Coad.

An international Champion: N. & S. Ch. PetiAmi's Devil's Rose, owned and bred by Wivi Anne Olson in Norway. Nordic winner 2008, Norwegian winner 2008, 3 times Best in Show (Int. NKK Championship Show, including jubilee Show 2008), and Top Dog (Bamsevinner) of all breeds in Norway in 2008.
Photo: Per Arnfinn Olsen.

Canadian and American Ch. Whitebreds Kissed by Kenningway ('The Prince'). Winner of Best Puppy In Show and Best In Show and achieved top five ranking in 2009. Bred by Karen Graeber, owned by Karen and Dr John Graeber (Whitebred Bichons), and Kendra James (Kenningway Bichons), and handled by Mr Anibal Faria.
Photo courtesy: Ashby Photography.

dogs ceased to be described as either "American" or "Continental".

It is interesting to note that there is now a much healthier uniformity of type, which exists around the world as a result of a much easier exchange of dogs from country to country. The difference in type here in the UK was quite significant in the past, probably as a direct result of the quarantine restrictions imposed on British breeders.

When judges are asked to judge our breed, the Breed Standard is adhered to carefully when deciding which of the dogs most closely resembles the perfect dog as described by the Standard. Naturally, because dogs are living, breathing creatures, and slight differences in appearance and behaviour can vary from one dog to another. However, the onus is on the breeder/exhibitor to present their dog to the Standard as closely as they can. So, for example, when the Standard states that the coat should be "soft, white and curly" then to breed a dog without this characteristic would be seen to be breeding away from breed type and would be penalised in the show ring.

ANALYSIS AND INTERPRETATION OF THE BREED STANDARDS

GENERAL APPEARANCE
FCI
1997 classification: group 9 Companion & Toy group.

Lively and Playful little dog with a lively gait, medium length of muzzle, long, loose corkscrew-curled hair very like the coat of a Mongolian goat. Head carriage is proud and high, with the eyes dark lively and expressive.

UK
1994 Classification: the Toy group. Well balanced dog of smart appearance, closely coated with handsome plume carried over the back. Natural white coat curling loosely. Head carriage proud and high.

USA
1988 Classification: The non-Sporting Group. The Bichon Frisé is a small sturdy white powder puff of a dog whose merry temperament is evidenced by his plumed tail carried jauntily over the back and his dark eyed inquisitive expression. This is a breed that has no gross or incapacitating exaggerations and therefore there is no inherent reason for lack of balance or unsound movement. Any deviation from the ideal described in the Standard should be penalised to the extent of the deviation. Structural faults common to all breeds are as undesirable in the Bichon Frisé as in any other breed, even though such faults may not be specifically mentioned in the Standard.

It is quite clear in all three

Standards that it is the coat that presents the major difference when listing a general overall appearance. All three use a quite different description to describe the coat: "ike a Mongolian goat" of the FCI is very much the natural state of the Bichon coat. This is how, until quite recently, dogs were exhibited in France, with virtually no preparation other that bathing and basic grooming. In the UK Standard a slightly less unkempt "closely coated, and natural, white coat curling loosely" is mentioned, but still no trimming of the body coat is accepted.

Compare these with the call for a "powder puff" description of the US, which, incidentally, can only be achieved by extensive bathing, blow-drying, brushing and trimming with virtually nothing natural about the result. This fundamental difference is instantly apparent when comparing the three Breed Standards.

CHARACTERISTICS
FCI
No separate description.

UK
Gay, happy, lively little dog.

USA
No separate description.

Only the UK Standard makes any reference to breed characteristics, which is unusual considering the Bichon really should be a happy

The Bichon is a sturdy, well-balanced dog, with a proud head carriage.

and lively dog. He would never be expected to be aloof or unapproachable, nor quiet or guarded in nature. Bichons have always been considered to be "clown-like", and it was these very characteristics that secured their popularity with the early sailors. One of the more amusing characteristics in particular, which is rarely seen in any other breed of dog, is the Bichon 'wave'. Dogs will often be seen to rear up on their hind legs and wave their front legs in a very distinctive fashion. It is a charming and very amusing trick, and should be seen as a typical characteristic of the breed. In the UK, a Bichon, particularly in the show ring, would be expected to display a lively and happy character and a dull and unhappy Bichon should not be expected to be placed well.

TEMPERAMENT

FCI
No reference at all other than the "Lively and playful" reference in the general characteristics.

UK
Friendly and outgoing.

USA
Gentle-mannered, sensitive, playful and affectionate. A

cheerful attitude is the hallmark of the breed and one should settle for nothing less.

A good temperament is paramount and a bad-tempered, aggressive or very nervous Bichon is quite unacceptable, but only the US Standard states this most important point.

HEAD & SKULL
FCI
Skull: Rather flat to the touch, although the coat makes it appear round. The skull longer than the muzzle. The muzzle must not be thick nor heavy, without however being snipy; the cheeks are flat and not very muscular. The furrow between the superciliary arches slightly visible. Nose is rounded, black, finely grained. Stop not very marked.

UK
Ration of muzzle length to skull length 3:5 on a head of the correct width and length. Lines drawn between the outer corners of the eyes and nose will create a near equilateral triangle. Whole head in balance with body. Muzzle not thick, heavy or snipy. Cheeks flat, not very strongly muscled. Stop moderate but definite, hollow between the eyebrows just visible. Skull slightly rounded, not coarse, with hair accentuating rounded appearance. Nose large, round, black soft and shiny.

This is an out-going dog, playful and affectionate.

USA
Skull slightly rounded allowing for a round and forward looking eye. The stop is slightly accentuated. Muzzle: a properly balanced head is three parts muzzle to five parts skull, measured from the nose to the occiput. A line drawn between the outside corners of the eyes and to the nose will create a near equilateral triangle. There is a slight degree of chiselling under the eyes, but not so much as to result in a weak and snipy foreface. The lower jaw is strong. The nose is prominent and always black.

All three Standards are quite specific when it comes to head properties and each in their way describes the very distinctive head of the Bichon well. The most common problem is a longer muzzle and narrow skull, which will give the dog a more Poodle-like head. These two

The typical expression of the Bichon is soft, yet also inquisitive and alert.

Eye size and colour have always been particularly difficult to assess and "not too big", "fairly large" and "overly large" when describing the size do little to make it any easier. These days, eyes are very rarely too big but are most likely to be smaller than is ideal when it comes to balancing the facial expression. Eye colour, too, is most difficult to assess. One person's evaluation of a "dark brown" eye would be much too light for another, making an accurate assessment of eye colour very difficult indeed.

faults can completely change the whole balance of the head by creating a more obliquely set eye.

EYES
FCI
Dark eyes as much as possible with dark eyelids, of a rather round shape and not almond-shaped; not placed obliquely; lively, not too big, not showing any white. Neither large nor prominent as in the Griffon Bruxellois and the Peke; the socket must not bulge. The eyeball must not stand out too much.

UK
Dark, round with black eye rims surrounded by dark haloes consisting of well pigmented skin. Forward looking, fairly large but not almond-shaped, neither obliquely set nor protruding. Showing no white when looking forward. Alert, full of expression.

USA
Soft, dark eyed, inquisitive, alert. Round black or dark brown and are set in the skull to look directly forward. An overly large or bulging eye is a fault as is the almond shaped obliquely set eye. Haloes, the black or very dark brown surrounding the eyes are necessary as they accentuate the eye and enhance expression. Broken pigment or total absence of pigment on the eye rims produces a blank and staring expression, which is a definite fault.

Eyes of any other colour than black or dark brown are a very serious fault and must be severely penalized.

EARS
FCI
Drooping, well furnished with fine curly long hairs, carried rather forward when the dog is attentive but in such a way that the front edge touches the skull and does not stand away obliquely; the length of the cartilage must, like in the Poodle, extend to the nose, but stop halfway of the length of the muzzle. They are anyway not as wide and are finer than the Poodle.

UK
Hanging close to the head, well covered with flowing hair longer than leathers, set on slightly higher than eye level and rather forward on skull. Carried forward when alert, forward edge touching skull. Leather reaching approximately halfway along muzzle.

USA

Ears are drooping and are covered with long flowing hair. When extended towards the nose, the leathers reach approximately halfway along the length of the muzzle. They are set on slightly higher than eye level and rather forward on the skull, so that when alert they serve to frame the face.

Both the FCI and the UK make reference to the front edge of the ears touching the skull and not flying outwards, but there is no mention of this in the US. The length of hair left on the ears after trimming, in reality, has produced a marked difference in later years. This was traditionally left quite long in the FCI countries, but in the UK and the US the hair is trimmed back quite severely to create more of a rounded appearance to the head

MOUTH
FCI
Bite normal, i.e. the incisors of the lower jaw are placed immediately against and behind the point of the teeth in the upper jaw. Lips are fine, rather lean, less however than in the Schipperke, falling only enough as to cover the lower lip, but never heavy or pendulous. They are normally black up to the corner of the lips, the lower lip must

not be heavy or visible, nor slack and does not allow the mucus membrane to be seen when the mouth is closed

UK
Jaws strong, with a perfect, regular and complete scissor bite, i.e. upper teeth closely overlapping lower teeth and set square to the jaws. Full dentition desirable. Lips fine, fairly tight and completely black.

USA
Bite is scissors. A bite, which is undershot, should be severely penalised. A crooked or out of line tooth is permissible:

The jaws should meet in a scissor bite with the teeth on the upper jaw closely overlapping the teeth on the lower jaw.

however missing teeth are to be severely penalised. Lips are black, fine and never drooping.

All three Standards demand black lips, but it is important to stress that the pigment should be unbroken, as is stated in both the FCI and UK Standards. Only the UK calls for a strong jawline, a breed point that has proved over the years to be so important if we are to continue to produce dogs with full dentition and correct bites. Weak and snipy jaws inevitably produce poor dentition and crooked teeth with little room for a correct bite to develop.

The US Standard goes as far as forgiving the odd crooked or out-of-line tooth but stresses the importance of full dentition.

NECK
FCI
Reach of neck is fairly long, carried high and proudly. Round and fine near the skull, broadening gradually to merge smoothly into the shoulders. Its length is approximately a third of the length of the body (proportion of 11 cm to 33 cm for the dog 27 cm high), the points of the shoulder blades against the withers taken as a basis.

UK
Arched neck, fairly long about one-third the length

of the body. Carried high and proudly. Round and slim near the head, gradually broadening to fit smoothly into shoulders.

USA

The arched neck is long and carried proudly behind an erect head; it blends smoothly into the shoulders. The length of the neck from occiput to withers is approximately one third the distance from the forechest to the buttocks.

The description of length of neck is described adequately by all three Standards with the FCI taking the description a little further by giving the proportions, making this a lot easier to understand and less open to misinterpretation

FOREQUARTERS
FCI

Seen from the front, forelegs really straight and perpendicular; fine bone. The shoulder is fairly slanted, not prominent, giving the appearance of being the same length as the upper arm, about 10 cm; does not stand away from the body and the elbow in particular does not turn out.

The legs are straight and perpendicular when viewed from the front.

Upper arm not standing away from the body. Elbow not turned out. Pastern short and straight seen from the front, very slightly oblique seen in profile.

UK

Shoulders oblique, not prominent, equal in length to upper arm. Upper arm fits close to body. Legs straight, perpendicular, when seen from front; not too finely boned. Pasterns short and straight viewed from front, very

slightly oblique viewed from side.

USA

The shoulder blade, upper arm and forearm are approximately equal in length. The shoulders are laid back to somewhat near a forty-five degree angle. The upper arm extends well back so the elbow is placed directly below the withers when viewed from the side. Legs are of medium bone, straight, with no bow or curve in the forearm or wrist. The elbows are held close to the body. The pasterns slope slightly from the vertical. The dewclaws may be removed.

The biggest difference here has to be the call for different types of bone, which I feel has always been at the very heart of the differences between Bichons from different countries. FCI calls for fine bone, the UK for not too finely boned, suggesting a little heavier than the FCI, and the US calling for medium bone, which would be heavier than ideal for our British Bichons that are in the Toy group.

BODY
FCI

Loin broad and well muscled, slightly arched. Rump: slightly rounded. Chest: well developed, the false ribs

rounded and do not end abruptly, the chest having horizontally a rather great depth.

UK

Fore chest well developed, deep brisket. Ribs well sprung, floating ribs not terminating abruptly. Loin broad, well muscled, slightly arched and well tucked up. Pelvis broad, croup slightly rounded. Length from withers to tailset should equal height from withers to ground.

USA

The chest is well developed and wide enough to allow free and unrestricted movement of the front legs. The lowest point of the chest extends at least to the elbow. The rib cage is moderately sprung and extends back to a short and muscular loin. The fore chest is well pronounced and protrudes slightly forward of the point of shoulder. The underline has a moderate tuck up.

Only the US Standard calls for the loin to be short, and this has also been one of the most obvious differences in the two main types of Bichon that will be seen. A shorter loin will produce an overall appearance of being shorter in the back, which will then compromise the UK's 'ideal' of length of withers to tailset equalling the height from withers to ground.

The length of the body from the withers to the tail-set should equal the height of the withers to the ground.

HINDQUARTERS

FCI

The pelvis is wide. Thighs: Broad and muscular; well slanting. Hocks: compared with the Poodle the hock joint is also more angulated.

UK

Thighs broad and well rounded. Stifles well bent; hocks well angulated and metatarsals perpendicular.

USA

The hindquarters are of medium bone, well angulated with muscular thighs and spaced moderately wide. The upper and lower thigh is nearly equal in length meeting at a well-bent stifle joint.

The thighs are broad and well-rounded.

The US Standard is more specific and actually mentions that the upper and lower thigh be nearly equal in length as well as being moderately spaced. One of the biggest faults in many dogs is that they are short in upper arm or upper thigh, resulting in being a little shorter in leg than is ideal for overall balance.

FEET
FCI
Sinewy. Nails preferably black; it is however an ideal, difficult to obtain.

UK
Tight, rounded and well knuckled up. Pads black. Nails preferably black.

USA
Feet are tight and round resembling those of a cat and point directly forward turning neither in nor out. Pads are black. Nails kept short.

The FCI Standard fails to mention black pads, which I feel is a serious omission. In my experience, a dog can be well pigmented in every other area of his body but still have incomplete pigmentation on his pads. This has to be regarded as a failing and be penalised as such.

TAIL
FCI
The tail is set a little more below the back line than the Poodle. Normally the tail is carried high and gracefully curved in line with the spine, without being rolled up; it is not docked and must not be in contact with the back; however, the tail furnishings may fall onto the back.

UK
Normally carried raised and curved gracefully over the back but not tightly curled. Never docked, carried in line with the backbone, only hair touching back; tail itself not in contact. Set on level with topline, neither too high nor too low. Corkscrew tail undesirable.

USA
Tail is well plumed, set on level with the topline and curved gracefully over the back so that the hair of the tail rests on the back. When the tail is extended towards the head it reaches at least halfway to the withers. A low set tail carried perpendicularly to the back, or a tail which droops behind, is to be severely penalized. A corkscrew tail is a serious fault.

Only the US Standard makes any reference to the actual length of the tail. Halfway to the withers is a fair description. Neither the FCI nor the UK Standard mentions the tail drooping behind, which is an extremely common occurrence. However, this is more of an indication of mood rather than a point of

The tail should curve gracefully over the back.

conformation. A dog is generally considered less likely to drop his tail behind him when he is relaxed or unhappy if the tail is set a little higher than in line with the backbone. A higher set tail will also make the dog appear a little shorter in back. These adjustments to the Standard may have their advantages when competing in the show ring, but should be penalised in the same way as a low set tail or a dog who appears too long in back.

GAIT AND MOVEMENT
FCI
Not mentioned separately.

UK
Balanced and effortless with an easy reach and drive maintaining a steady topline. Legs moving straight along the line of travel, with hind pads showing.

USA
Movement at a trot is free, precise and effortless. In profile the forelegs and hindlegs extend equally with an easy reach and drive that maintains a steady topline. When moving, the head and neck remain somewhat erect and as speed increases there is a very slight convergence of legs towards the centre line. Moving away, the hindquarters travel with moderate width between

them and the footpads can be seen. Coming and going his movement is precise and true.

I find it surprising that there is no mention of gait and movement in the FCI Standard at this point. The UK and USA descriptions are much the same with the USA taking it a little further and calling for some width to the hindquarters, which is a particularly valid point. Many Bichons can appear quite narrow on the rear, which can make them move very close behind.

The USA Standard also refers to head carriage again when on

Movement is balanced and effortless.

the move, although the only reference to this in the UK and FCI Standards is within the description of the neck.

COAT
FCI
Fine silky, very loose corkscrew curls looking like the coat (fur) of the Mongolian goat, neither flat nor corded and 7 to 10 cm long. The dog may be shown with feet and muzzle slightly tidied up.

UK
Fine, silky, with soft corkscrew curls, neither flat nor corded and measuring 7 to 10 cm in length. The dog may be presented untrimmed or have the muzzle and feet slightly tidied up.

USA
The texture of the coat is of utmost importance. The undercoat is soft and dense, the outer coat of a coarser and curlier texture. The combination of the two gives a soft but substantial feel to the touch which is similar to plush or velvet and when patted, springs back. When bathed and brushed, it stands off the body, creating an overall powder puff appearance. A wiry coat is not desirable. A limp, silky coat that lies down or a lack of undercoat, are

The coat is silky in texture with soft corkscrew curls.

serious faults. Trimming: the coat is trimmed to reveal the natural outline of the body. It is rounded off from any direction and never cut so short as to create an over-trimmed or squared off appearance. The furnishings of the head, beard, moustache, ears and tail are left longer. The longer head hair is trimmed to create an overall rounded impression. The topline is trimmed to appear level. The coat is long enough to maintain the powder puff look which is characteristic to the breed.

The FCI Standard forbids any kind of trimming and officials and exhibitors, particularly in France, have strongly resisted any attempts to successfully exhibit a trimmed dog. However, one by one, the neighbouring countries have presented their Bichons in a similar way to the rest of the world and, quite recently, an exhibitor from the UK won a very high award under a French Judge with a Bichon who was trimmed. As I have mentioned before, the borders have opened up because dogs can now travel freely around Europe and so Bichons are now being exhibited and judged to the FCI Standard fully trimmed.

The UK breeders have always

The colour is pure white, but you may see cream or apricot markings on puppies.

deliberately ignored this part of our Standard and presented all our dogs trimmed, but have preferred a slightly longer style than the USA.

COLOUR
FCI
Pure white. The pigmentation beneath the white coat is preferably dark; the genitals are then pigmented, either black, bluish or beige.

UK
White, but cream or apricot markings acceptable up to 18 months. Under white coat, dark pigment desirable. Black blue or beige markings often found on skin.

USA
Colour is white, may have shadings of buff cream or apricot around the ears or on the body. Any excess of 10 per cent of the entire coat of a mature specimen is a fault and should be penalized, but colour of the accepted shading should not be faulted in puppies.

The UK and FCI Standard will not accept any colour in the coat past 18 months of age. These Standards mention that pigment can be black, blue or beige although, in my experience, beige pigment will never be favoured as highly as black pigment. Pigment has always varied according to the time of year, and I think it is worth noting that depth of pigment improves considerably during the summer months.

SIZE
FCI
The height at the withers should not exceed 30 cm, the small size being an element of success.

The height stipulation is the same for both males and females.

UK
Ideal height 23-28cms (9-11 in) at withers.

USA
Dogs and bitches 9.5 to 11.5 inches are to be given primary preference. Only where the comparative superiority of a specimen outside this range clearly justifies it should greater latitude be taken. In no case should this latitude extend over 12 inches or under 9 inches. The minimum limits do not apply to puppies.

Although each Standard is quite specific about the size ranges and its acceptable limits, I feel it is worth pointing out that, as a Toy breed, the Bichon should be a small dog. For a while the UK Standard included the same line that is present in the FCI Standard: "the small size being the element of success". When comparing the Standards at this point, we have to appreciate that a "finely boned" 9-in (23-cm) Bichon, bred to the FCI Standard, is going to look quite different in overall size to a medium-boned 12-in (30-cm) dog, bred to the USA Standard.

FAULTS
FCI
- **Slightly overshot or undershot mouth**
- **Pigmentation extending into the coat and forming rusty patches. Coat flat, wavy or too short.**

ELIMINATING FAULTS

- Pink nose. Flesh coloured lips. Light coloured eyes. Prognathism (undershot-overshot) so developed to the extent that the incisors do not touch. Rolled up tail or twisted into a spiral. Black spots in the coat.
- Male animals should have two apparently normal testicles fully descended into the scrotum.

UK

Male animals should have two apparently normal testicles fully descended into the scrotum.

Any departure from the foregoing points should be considered a fault and the seriousness with which each fault be regarded should be in exact proportion to its degree.

USA

Faults are included in each clause of the American standard but there is no reference regarding testicles.

Only the FCI Standard gives a

The Breed Standard describes the 'perfect' Bichon, but this must also be open to the judge's individual interpretation.

list of faults. However, I feel the UK Standard covers this aspect very well. Assessing faults will always be a question of degree. Other than the few serious faults such as, an undershot jaw, monorchid or cryptorchid, aggressive or very nervous, most faults are a matter of what is acceptable or unacceptable to the person who is judging. No two judges will interpret a Standard in the same way and this is fine, providing the essence of the breed is understood.

HAPPY AND HEALTHY

Chapter

8

The Bichon Frisé is a toy breed with great character. In my experience, the Bichon is rather like a big dog trying to escape from a small body!

The Bichon has a good life-span which can run well into double figures, provided his needs are met. He is a real character, a plucky and faithful companion, a willing friend on a non-conditional basis. He will, however, of necessity rely on you for food and shelter, accident prevention, and medication. A healthy Bichon is a happy chap with a waggy tail, looking to please and amuse his owner.

There are a few genetic conditions that occur in the Bichon which will be covered in depth later in the chapter, but generally, this is a healthy dog with a zest for life.

VACCINATION

There is much debate over the issue of vaccination at the moment. Timing of the final part of the initial vaccination course for a puppy, and the frequency of subsequent booster vaccinations, are both under scrutiny. Some manufacturers have vaccines against certain diseases licensed for use every three years, after the initial course. An evaluation of the relative risk for each disease plays a part, depending on the local situation.

Many owners think that the actual vaccination is the protection, so that their puppy can go out for walks as soon as he or she has had the final part of the puppy vaccination course. This is not the case.

The rationale behind vaccination is to stimulate the immune system into producing protective antibodies, which will be triggered if the patient is subsequently exposed to that particular disease. This means that a further one or two weeks will have to pass before an effective level of protection will have developed.

Vaccines against viruses stimulate longer-lasting protection than those against bacteria, whose effect may only persist for a matter of months in some cases. There is also the possibility of an individual failing to mount a full immune response to a vaccination: although the vaccine schedule may have been followed as recommended, that particular dog remains vulnerable.

As in human medicine, adverse reactions to vaccination can occur, albeit rarely, and must be weighed against the advantages of protection against serious, sometimes potentially life-threatening, diseases.

An individual's level of protection against rabies, as

Your Bichon can be given a check-up when he goes for a booster injection.

leptospirosis; a decision to vaccinate against one or more non-core diseases will be based on an individual's level of risk, determined on lifestyle and where you live in the US.

Do remember, however, that the booster visit to the veterinary surgery is not 'just' for a booster. I am regularly correcting my clients when they announce that they have 'just' brought their pet for a booster. Instead, this appointment is a chance for a full health-check and evaluation of how a particular dog is doing. After all, we are all conversant with the addage that a human year is equivalent to seven canine years.

There have been attempts in recent times to re-set the scale for two reasons: small breeds live longer than giant breeds, and dogs are living longer than previously. I have seen dogs of 17 and 18 years of age but to say a dog is 119 or 126 years old is plainly meaningless. It does emphasise the fact, though, that a dog's health can change dramatically over the course of a single year because dogs age at a far greater rate than humans.

For me as a veterinary surgeon, the booster vaccination visit is a challenge: how much can I find of which the owner was unaware, such as rotten teeth or a heart murmur? Even monitoring bodyweight year upon year is of use because bodyweight can creep up, or down, without an owner realising. Being overweight is unhealthy, but it may take an outsider's remark to make an owner realise that there is a

demonstrated by the antibody titre in a blood sample, is routinely tested in the UK in order to fulfil the requirements of the Pet Travel Scheme (PETS). This is not the case with other individual diseases in order to gauge the need for booster vaccination or to determine the effect of a course of vaccines; instead, your veterinary surgeon will advise a protocol based upon the vaccines available, local disease prevalence, and the lifestyle of you and your dog.

It is worth remembering that maintaining a fully effective level of immune protection against the disease appropriate to your locale is vital: these are serious diseases which may result in the demise of your dog, and some may have the potential to be passed on to his human family (so-called zoonotic potential for transmission). This is where you will be grateful for your veterinary surgeon's own knowledge and advice.

The American Animal Hospital Association laid down guidance at the end of 2006 for the vaccination of dogs in North America. Core diseases were defined as distemper, adenovirus, parvovirus and rabies. So-called non-core diseases are kennel cough, Lyme disease and

Kennel Cough is highly contagious and will spread rapidly among dogs that live together.

problem. Conversely, a drop in bodyweight may be the only pointer to an underlying problem.

The diseases against which dogs are vaccinated include:

ADENOVIRUS

Canine Adenovirus 1 (CAV-1) affects the liver (hepatitis) and causes the classic 'blue eye' appearance in some affected dogs, while CAV-2 is a cause of kennel cough (see later). Vaccines often include both canine adenoviruses.

DISTEMPER

Also called 'hardpad' from the characteristic changes to the pads of the paws, distemper has a worldwide distribution, but fortunately vaccination has been very effective at reducing its occurrence. It is caused by a virus and affects the respiratory, gastro-intestinal (gut) and nervous systems, so it causes a wide range of illnesses. Fox and urban stray dog populations are most at risk, and therefore responsible for local outbreaks.

KENNEL COUGH

Also known as infectious tracheobronchitis – *Bordetella bronchiseptica* is not only a major cause of kennel cough but also a common secondary infection on top of another cause. Being a bacterium, it is susceptible to treatment with appropriate antibiotics, but the immunity stimulated by the vaccine is therefore short-lived (six to 12 months).

This vaccine is often in a form to be administered down the nostrils in order to stimulate local immunity at the point of entry, so to speak. Do not be alarmed to see your veterinary surgeon using needle and syringe to draw up the vaccine because the needle will be replaced with a special plastic introducer, allowing the vaccine to be gently instilled into each nostril. Dogs generally resent being held more than the actual intra-nasal vaccine, and I have learnt that covering the patient's eyes helps greatly.

127

Kennel cough is, however, rather a catch-all term for any cough spreading within a dog population, not just in kennels but also between dogs at a training session or breed show, or even mixing out in the park. Many of these infections may not be *B. bronchiseptica* but other viruses, for which one can only treat symptomatically.

Parainfluenza virus is often included in a vaccine programme because it is a common viral cause of kennel cough.

Kennel cough can seem alarming. There is a persistent cough accompanied by production of white frothy spittle which can last for a matter of weeks, during which time the patient is highly infectious to other dogs. I remember when it ran through our five Border Collies – there were white patches of froth on the floor wherever you looked! Other features include sneezing, a runny nose, and eyes sore with conjunctivitis. Fortunately, these infections are generally self-limiting, most dogs recovering without any long-lasting problems, but an elderly dog may be knocked sideways by it, akin to the effects of a common cold on a frail elderly person.

LEPTOSPIROSIS

This disease is caused by *Leptospira interogans*, a spiral-shaped bacterium. There are several natural variants or serovars. Each is characteristically found in one or more particular host animal species, which then acts as a reservoir, intermittently shedding leptospires in the urine. Infection can also be picked up at mating, via bite wounds, across the placenta, or through eating the carcases of infected animals, such as rats.

A serovar will cause actual clinical disease in an individual when two conditions are fulfilled: the individual is not the natural host species, and is also not immune to that particular serovar.

Leptospirosis is a zoonotic disease, known as Weil's disease in humans, with implications for all those in contact with an affected dog. It is also commonly called rat jaundice, reflecting the rat's important role as a reservoir of *Leptospira icterohaemorrhagiae* to both humans and dogs. The UK National Rodent Survey 2003 found a wild brown rat population of 60 million, equivalent at the time to one rat per person. This means that there is as much a risk for the Bichon living with a family in a town as the Bichon leading a more rural lifestyle.

Signs of illness reflect the organs affected by a particular serovar. In man, there may be a flu-like illness or a more serious, often life-threatening disorder involving major body organs.

The illness in a susceptible dog may be mild, the dog recovering within two to three weeks without treatment but going on to develop long-term liver or

Both town and country dwellers are equally at risk from Leptosprirosis.

128

kidney disease. In contrast, peracute illness may result in a rapid deterioration and death following initial malaise and fever. There may also be anorexia, vomiting, diarrhoea, abdominal pain, joint pain, increased thirst and rate of urination, jaundice, and ocular changes. Haemorrhage is a common feature because of low platelet numbers, manifesting as bleeding under the skin, nose-bleeds (epistaxis), and the presence of blood in the urine and faeces (haematuria and melaena respectively).

I will never forget the 21-month-old Cocker Spaniel presented one Saturday morning simply because she had been quiet and off her food for three days. She had not been vaccinated since her second puppy vaccine at four-months-old. I found her to be running a fever of 41 degrees Centigrade, her gums were very pale, and her abdomen very painful. As I carried her out to the hospital area to take a blood sample, she passed a large volume of red urine... and died. There was also the group of unvaccinated dogs living on a poultry farm who died over the course of three weeks.

Treatment requires rigorous intra-venous fluid therapy to support the kidneys. Being a bacterial infection, it is possible to treat leptospirosis with specific antibiotics, although a prolonged course of several weeks is needed in order to avoid the development of the chronic carrier state. Strict hygiene and

barrier nursing are needed in order to avoid onward transmission of leptospirosis.

Vaccination reduces the severity of disease, but cannot prevent the development of chronic carrier state following exposure. There is little or no cross-protection between serovars. This means that vaccination will result in protection against only those serovars included in that particular vaccination. In the UK, vaccines have classically included L icterohaemorrhagiae (rat-adapted serovar) and L canicola (dog-specific serovar). The latter is of particular significance to us humans, since disease will not be apparent in an infected dog but leptospires will be shed intermittently.

The situation in the US is less

clear-cut. Blanket vaccination against leptospirosis is not considered necessary because it only occurs in certain areas. There has also been a shift in the serovars implicated in clinical disease, reflecting the effectiveness of vaccination and the migration of wildlife reservoirs carrying different serovars from rural areas, so you must be guided by your veterinarian's knowledge of the local situation.

LYME DISEASE

This is a bacterial infection transmitted by hard ticks. It is therefore found in those specific areas of the US where ticks are found such as north-eastern states, some southern states, California and the upper Mississippi region. It does also

Fortunately Lyme disease is still rare in the UK.

RABIES

This is another zoonotic disease and there are very strict control measures in place. Vaccines were once available in the UK only on an individual basis for dogs being taken abroad. Pets travelling into the UK had to serve six months' compulsory quarantine, so that any pet incubating rabies would be identified before release back into the general population. Under the Pet Travel Scheme (PETS), provided certain criteria are met (check the DEFRA website for up-to-date information), dogs can re-enter the UK without being quarantined.

Dogs to be imported into the US have to show that they were vaccinated against rabies at least 30 days previously, otherwise, they have to serve effective internal quarantine for 30 days from the date of vaccination against rabies, in order to ensure they are not incubating the disease. The exception is dogs entering from countries recognised as being rabies-free, in which case it has to be proved that they lived in that country for at least six months beforehand.

occur in the UK, but at a low level so vaccination is not routinely offered.

Clinical disease is manifested primarily as limping, due to arthritis, but other organs affected include the heart, kidneys and nervous system. It is readily treatable with appropriate antibiotics, once diagnosed, but the causal bacterium, *Borrelia burgdorferi*, is not cleared from the body totally and will persist.

Prevention requires both vaccination and tick control, especially as there are other diseases transmitted by ticks. Ticks carrying *B. burgdorferi* will transmit it to humans as well, but an infected dog cannot pass it to a human.

CANINE PARVOVIRUS (CPV)

Canine Parvovirus disease first appeared in the late 1970s when it was feared that the UK's dog population would be decimated by it because of the lack of immunity in the general canine population. This was a notion that terrified me at the time but which did not fortunately happen on the scale envisaged.

There are two forms of the virus (CPV-1, CPV-2) affecting domesticated dogs. CPV-2 also affects wild dogs. The virus is highly contagious, picked up via the mouth/nose from infected faeces. The incubation period is about five days.

CPV-2 causes two types of illness: gastro-enteritis (vomiting, haemorrhagic diarrhoea, fever)

and heart disease in puppies born to unvaccinated dams (myocarditis or inflammation of the cardiac muscle, heart failure, respiratory distress, diarrhoea), both of which often result in death.

Infection of puppies less than three weeks of age with CPV-1 manifests as diarrhoea, vomiting, difficulty breathing, and fading puppy syndrome. CPV-1 can cause abortion and fetal abnormalities in breeding bitches.

There is no specific treatment for CPV, the mainstay being aggressive fluid therapy coupled with anti-emetic drugs to counteract vomiting, and antibiotic cover because of the marked reduction in white blood cell numbers caused by the virus. In the convalescent period, an easily digested diet is essential, with low fibre content, while the lining of the gastro-intestinal tract recovers.

The virus is able to survive for several months in the environment. Although resistant to most disinfectants, it is susceptible to sodium hypochlorite at a dilution rate of 1:30 bleach to water.

Occurrence is mainly low now, thanks to vaccination against CPV-2. There is no vaccine available for CPV-1. The disease is more often mild or sub-clinical, with recovery more likely, although a recent outbreak in my area did claim the lives of several puppies and dogs. It is also occasionally seen in the elderly unvaccinated dog.

PARASITES

A parasite is defined as an organism deriving benefit on a one-way basis from another, the host. It goes without saying that it is not to the parasite's advantage to harm the host to such an extent that the benefit is lost, especially if it results in the death of the host.

This means a dog could harbour parasites, internal and/or external, without there being any signs apparent to the owner. Many canine parasites can, however, transfer to humans with variable consequences, so routine preventative treatment is advised against particular parasites. Just as with vaccination, risk assessment plays a part – for example, there is no need for routine heartworm treatment in the UK (at present), but it is vital in the US and in Mediterranean countries.

ROUNDWORMS (NEMATODES)

These are the spaghetti-like worms, which you may have been unfortunate enough to have seen passed in faeces or brought up in vomit. Most of the de-worming treatments in use today cause the adults roundworms to disintegrate, thankfully, so that treating puppies in particular is not as unpleasant as it used to be!

Most puppies will have a worm burden, mainly of a particular roundworm species (*Toxocara canis*), which reactivates within the dam's tissues during pregnancy and passes to the fetuses developing in the womb.

The breeder will have started a worming programme which you will need to continue.

It is therefore important to treat the dam both during and after pregnancy, as well as the puppies.

Professional advice is to continue worming every one to three months. There are roundworm eggs in the environment and, unless you examine your dog's faeces under a microscope on a very regular basis for the presence of roundworm eggs, you will be unaware of your dog having picked up roundworms, unless he should have such a heavy burden that he passes the adults.

It takes a few weeks from the time that a dog swallows a *Toxocara canis* roundworm egg to himself passing viable eggs (the pre-patent period). These eggs are not immediately infective to other animals, requiring a period of maturation in the environment, which is primarily temperature dependent and therefore shorter in the summer (as little as two weeks) than in the winter (several months). It is worth noting that the eggs can survive in the environment for two years and more.

There are deworming products which are active all the time, which will provide continuous protection when administered as often as directed. Otherwise, treating every month will, in effect, cut in before a dog could theoretically become a source of roundworm eggs to the general population.

It is the risk to human health which is so important: *T. canis* roundworms will migrate within our tissues and cause all manner of problems, not least of which (but fortunately rarely) is blindness. The incidence in humans has fallen dramatically in recent years. If a dog has roundworms, the eggs also find their way onto his coat where they can be picked up during stroking and cuddling. Sensible hygiene is therefore important.

You should always carefully pick up your dog's faeces and dispose of them appropriately, thereby preventing the

maturation of any eggs present in the fresh faeces. This will not only reduce the chance for environmental contamination with all manner of infections but also make walking more pleasant underfoot.

TAPEWORMS (CESTODES)

When considering the general dog population, the primary source of the most common tapeworm species will be fleas, which can carry the eggs. Most multi-wormers will be active against these tapeworms, not because they are a hazard to human health but because it is

unpleasant to see the wriggly rice grain tapeworm segments emerging from your dog's back passage while he is lying in front of the fire, and usually when you have guests for dinner.

A tapeworm of significance to human health is *Echinococcus granulosus*, found in a few parts of the UK, mainly in Wales. Man is an intermediate host for this tapeworm, along with sheep, cattle and pigs. Inadvertent ingestion of eggs passed in the faeces of an infected dog is followed by the development of so called hydatid cysts in major organs such as the lungs and

HEARTWORM (DIROFILARIA IMMITIS)

Heartworm infection has been diagnosed in dogs all over the world. There are two prerequisites: presence of mosquitoes, and a warm humid climate.

When a female mosquito bites an infected animal, it acquires *D. immitis* in its circulating form, as microfilariae. A warm environmental temperature is needed for these microfilariae to develop into the infective third-stage larvae (L3) within the mosquitoes, the so-called intermediate host. L3 larvae are then transmitted by the mosquito when it next bites a dog. Therefore, while heartworm infection is found in all the states of the US, it is at differing levels such that an occurrence in Alaska, for example, is probably a reflection of a visiting dog having previously picked up the infection elsewhere.

Heartworm infection is not currently a problem in the UK, except for those dogs contracting it while abroad without suitable

preventative treatment. Global warming and its effect on the UK's climate, however, could change that.

It is a potentially life-threatening condition, with dogs of all breeds and ages being susceptible without preventative treatment. The larvae can grow to 14 inches within the right side of the heart, causing primarily signs of heart failure and ultimately liver and kidney damage. It can be treated but prevention is a better plan. In the US, regular blood tests for the presence of infection are advised, coupled with appropriate preventative measures, so I would advise liaison with your veterinary surgeon.

For dogs travelling to heartworm-endemic areas of the EU such as the Mediterranean coast, preventative treatment should be started before leaving the UK and maintained during the visit. Again, this is best arranged with your veterinary surgeon.

liver, necessitating surgical removal. Dogs become infected through eating raw meat containing hydatid cysts. Cooking will kill hydatid cysts, so general advice is to avoid feeding raw meat and offal in areas of high risk.

There are specific requirements for treatment with praziquantel within 24 to 48 hours of return into the UK under the PETS. This is to prevent the inadvertent introduction of *Echinococcus multilocularis*, a tapeworm carried by foxes on mainland Europe, which is transmissible to humans, causing serious or even fatal liver disease.

FLEAS

There are several species of flea, which are not host-specific: not only can a dog be carrying cat and human fleas as well as dog fleas, but also the same flea treatment will kill and/or control them all. It is also accepted that environmental control is a vital part of a flea control programme. This is because the adult flea is only on the animal for as long as it takes to have a blood meal and to breed; the remainder of the life cycle occurs in the house, car, caravan, shed...

There is a vast array of flea control products available, with various routes of administration: collar, powder, spray, 'spot-on', oral. Since flea control needs to

Spot on treatment is effective in preventing infestation from fleas.

be applied to all pets in the house, irrespective of whether they leave the house (since fleas can be introduced into the house by other pets and their human owners), it is best to discuss your specific flea control needs with your veterinary surgeon.

MITES

There are five types of mite which can affect dogs:

i. Demodex canis: This mite is a normal inhabitant of canine hair follicles, passed from the bitch to her pups as they suckle. The development of actual skin disease or demodicosis depends on the individual. It is seen frequently around the time of puberty and after a bitch's first season, associated with hormonal changes. There may, however, be an inherited weakness in an individual's immune system

enabling multiplication of the mite. The localised form consists of areas of fur loss without itchiness, generally around the face and on the forelimbs, and 90 per cent will recover without treatment.

The other 10 per cent develop the juvenile-onset generalised form, of which half will recover spontaneously. The other half may be depressed, go off their food, and show signs of itchiness due to secondary bacterial skin infections. Treatment is often prolonged over several months and consists of regular bathing with a specific miticidal shampoo, often clipping away fur to improve access to the skin, together with a suitable antibiotic by mouth. There is also now a licensed 'spot-on' preparation available. Progress is monitored by examination of deep skin scrapings for the presence of the mite; the initial diagnosis is based upon abnormally high numbers of the mite, often with live individuals being seen.

There is a third group of individuals developing demodicosis for the first time in middle-age (more than about four years of age), and as the generalised form. This is often reflecting underlying immunosuppression by an internal disease process, such as neoplasia, or treatment with corticosteroids, for example, so it is important to identify any predisposing cause and correct it where possible, as well as specifically treating as above.

(ii) Sarcoptes scabei: This mite characteristically causes an intense pruritus or itchiness in the affected dog, causing the dog to incessantly scratch and bite at himself, leading to marked fur loss and skin trauma. Initially starting on the elbows, ear flaps and hocks, without treatment the skin on the rest of the body can become involved, with thickening and pigmentation of the skin. Secondary bacterial infections are common.

Unlike *Demodex*, this mite lives at the skin surface, and it can be hard to find in skin scrapings. It is therefore not unusual to treat a patient for sarcoptic mange (scabies) based on the appearance of the problem even with negative skin scraping findings, and especially if there is a history of contact with foxes, which are a frequent source of the scabies mite. It will spread between dogs and can therefore also be found in situations where large numbers of dogs from different backgrounds are mixing together. It should be noted that it will cause itchiness in humans, although the mite cannot complete its life cycle on us, so

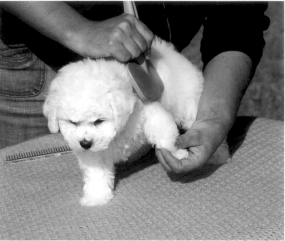

A Bichon puppy must get used to a routine of regular grooming as a close check should be kept on the skin once the adult coat comes through.

treating all affected dogs should be sufficient.

Fortunately, there is now a highly effective 'spot-on' treatment for Sarcoptes scabei.

(iii) Cheyletiella yasguri: This is the fur mite most commonly found on dogs. It is often called 'walking dandruff' because it can be possible to see collections of the small white mite moving about over the skin surface. There is excessive scale and dandruff formation, and mild itchiness. It is important as a zoonosis, being transmissible to humans where it causes a pruritic rash.

Diagnosis is by microscopic examination of skin scrapings, coat combings and sticky tape impressions from the skin and fur. Treatment is with an

appropriate insecticide, as advised by your veterinary surgeon.

(iv) Otodectes cynotis: A highly transmissible otitis externa (outer ear infection) results from the presence in the outer ear canal of this ear mite, characterised by exuberant production of dark ear wax. The patient will frequently shake his head and rub at the ear(s) affected. The mites can also spread to the skin adjacent to the opening of the external ear canal, and may transfer elsewhere, such as to the paws.

When using an otoscope to examine the outer ear canal, the heat from the light source will often cause any ear mites present to start moving around. I often offer owners the chance to have a look because it really is quite an extraordinary sight! It is also possible to identify the mite from ear wax smeared onto a slide and examined under a microscope.

Cats are a common source of ear mites. It is not unusual to find ear mites during the routine examination of puppies and kittens. Treatment options include specific ear drops acting against both the mite and any secondary infections present in the auditory canal, and certain 'spot-on' formulations. It is vital to treat all dogs and cats in the household to prevent re-cycling of the mite between individuals.

(v) The free-living mite (Neo-Trombicula autumnalis) or harvest mite: This mite can cause an intense local irritation on the skin. Its larvae are picked up from undergrowth, so they are characteristically found as a bright orange patch on the web of skin between the digits of the paws. It feeds on skin cells before dropping off to complete its life cycle in the environment.

Its name is a little misleading because it is not restricted to the autumn nor to harvest-time; I find it on the ear flaps of cats from late June onwards, depending on the prevailing weather. It will also bite humans. Treatment depends on identifying and avoiding hotspots for picking up harvest mite, if possible. Checking the skin (especially the paws) after exercise, and mechanically removing any mites found will reduce the chances of irritation, which can be treated symptomatically. Insecticides can also be applied – be guided by your veterinary surgeon.

Get into the habit of checking your Bichon all over when he has returned from exercise – particularly if you live in a rural area.

TICKS

There were said to be classic pockets of ticks in the UK, such as the New Forest and Thetford Forest, but they are actually found nationwide. The lifecycle is curious: each life stage takes a year to develop and move on to the next. Long grass is a major habitat. The vibration of animals moving through the grass will stimulate the larva, nymph or adult to climb up a blade of grass and wave its legs in the air as it 'quests' for a host on to which to latch for its next blood meal. Humans are as likely to be hosts, so ramblers and orienteers are advised to cover their legs when going through rough long grass, tucking the ends of their trousers into their socks.

As well as their physical presence causing irritation, it is the potential for disease transmission that is of concern. A tick will transmit any infection previously contracted while feeding on an animal: for example *Borrelia burgdorferi*, the causal agent of Lyme disease (see page 129). There are highly effective insecticides available.

A-Z OF COMMON AILMENTS

ANAL SACS (IMPACTED)
The anal sacs lie on either side of the back passage or anus, at approximately four- and eight-o'-clock, if compared with the face of a clock. They fill with a particularly pungent fluid, which is emptied onto the faeces as they move past the sacs to exit from the anus. Theories abound as to why these sacs should become impacted periodically and seemingly more so in some dogs than others. The irritation of impacted anal sacs is often seen as 'scooting', when the back side is dragged along the ground. Some dogs will gnaw at their back feet or over the rump.

Increasing the fibre content of the diet helps some dogs; in others, there is underlying skin disease. It may be a one-off occurrence for no apparent reason. Sometimes, an infection can become established, requiring antibiotic therapy which may need to be coupled with flushing out the infected sac under sedation or general anaesthesia. More rarely, a dog will present with an apparently acute-onset anal sac abscess, which is incredibly painful.

DIARRHOEA
Cause and treatment much as *Gastritis* (see below).

EAR INFECTIONS
The dog has a long external ear canal, initially vertical then horizontal, leading to the

CUSHING'S SYNDROME

As your Bichon grows older, you may notice the coat become harsh and wiry in nature. This is usually a perfectly normal ageing change. In some circumstances, however, changes in the coat may be a sign of underlying disease.

For example, the high levels of circulating cortisol occurring with Cushing's syndrome (otherwise called hyperadrenocorticism) result in characteristic changes in behaviour and appearance. This is one of the most common endocrine or hormonal disorders occurring in the dog. It may therefore be suspected early on when the signs are few and mild, such as a change in the coat, and it can be hard to diagnose definitively at this stage.

With time, more of the possible signs are likely. The owner may notice a ravenous appetite together with drinking far more water than usual and an increased need to urinate, possibly with a break in house-training or even urinary incontinence. Other possible behavioural changes include lethargy and reduced ability to exercise, often coupled with laboured breathing or panting. The owner of a Bichon with Cushing's syndrome may also notice a pot-bellied appearance and thinning or loss of fur on the flanks (often culminating in the classic bilateral flank alopoecia). The skin of the ventral abdomen or undercarriage may seem thin, with superficial blood vessels becoming easier to see, and blackheads often occur. Recurrent skin infections may occur, and any wounds or surgical incision may heal slower than anticipated. An unspayed bitch with Cushing's syndrome may no longer come into season.

Diagnosis involves blood tests, and examination of a urine sample, together with radiography and ultrasonography. Medical and surgical treatments are available, depending on the type of Cushing's syndrome detected.

eardrum which protects the middle ear. If your Bichon is shaking his head, then his ears will need to be inspected with an auroscope by a veterinary surgeon in order to identify any cause, and to ensure the eardrum is intact. A sample may be taken from the canal, to be examined under the microscope and cultured to identify causal agents, before prescribing appropriate ear drops containing antibiotic, anti-fungal agent and/or steroid. Predisposing causes of otitis externa or infection in the external ear canal include:

- Presence of a foreign body, such as a grass awn
- Ear mites, which are intensely irritating to the dog and stimulate the production of brown wax, predisposing to infection
- Previous infections causing the canal's lining to thicken
- Narrowing of the canal and reducing ventilation
- Water trapped in the external ear canal can lead to infection – the Bichon rarely likes swimming, but care should be taken when bathing him.

The Bichon's ears may not be very visible when a dog has a full coat, but they stil need regular checking and cleaning.

FOREIGN BODIES

Internal: Items swallowed in haste without checking whether they will be digested can cause problems if they lodge in the stomach or obstruct the intestines, necessitating surgical removal. Acute vomiting is the main indication. Common objects I have seen removed include stones from the garden, peach stones, babies' dummies,

golf balls, and once a lady's bra...

It is possible to diagnose a dog with an intestinal obstruction across a waiting room from a particularly 'tucked-up' stance and pained facial expression. These patients bounce back from surgery dramatically. A previously docile and compliant obstructed patient will return for a post-operative check-up and literally bounce into the consulting room.

External: Grass awns are adept at finding their way into orifices such as a nostril, down an ear, and into the soft skin between two digits (toes), whence they start a one-way journey due to the direction of their whiskers. In particular, I remember a grass awn which migrated from a

hindpaw, causing abscesses along the way but not yielding itself up until it erupted through the skin in the groin!

GASTRITIS

This is usually a simple stomach upset, most commonly in response to dietary indiscretion. Scavenging constitutes a change in the diet as much as an abrupt switch in the food being fed by the owner. There are also some specific infections causing more severe gastritis/enteritis which will require treatment from a veterinary surgeon (See also *Canine Parvovirus* under 'Vaccination' earlier).

Generally, a day without food followed by a few days of small, frequent meals of a bland diet, such as cooked chicken or fish or an appropriate prescription diet, should allow the stomach to settle. It is vital to ensure the patient is drinking and retaining sufficient to cover losses resulting from the stomach upset in addition to the normal losses to be expected when healthy. This is especially so with a small dog like the Bichon. Oral rehydration fluid may not be very appetising for the patient, in which case cooled boiled water should be offered instead. Fluids should initially be offered in small but frequent amounts to avoid over-drinking, which can result in further vomiting and thereby dehydration and electrolyte imbalances.

It is also important to gradually wean the patient back onto routine food or else another bout of gastritis may occur.

The Bichon is naturally active and athletic, so if you see signs of lameness or stiffness, consult a vet.

JOINT PROBLEMS

It is not unusual for older Bichons to be stiff after exercise, particularly in cold weather. Your veterinary surgeon will be able to advise you on ways for helping your dog cope with stiffness, not least of which will be to ensure that he is not overweight. Arthritic joints do not need to be burdened with extra bodyweight!

LUMPS AND BUMPS

Regularly handling and stroking your dog will enable the early detection of lumps and bumps, and is particularly important in the Bichon because of the profuse fur coat. These may be due to infection (abscess), bruising, multiplication of particular cells from within the body, or even an external parasite (tick). If you are worried about any lump you find, have it checked by a veterinary surgeon.

OBESITY

Being overweight does predispose to many other problems such as diabetes mellitus, heart disease and joint problems. It is so easily prevented by simply acting as your Bichon's conscience. Ignore pleading eyes and feed according to your dog's waistline. The body condition is what matters qualitatively, alongside monitoring that individual's bodyweight as a quantitative measure. The Bichon should, in my opinion as a health professional, have at least a suggestion of a waist beneath that lovely coat, and it should be possible to feel the ribs beneath only a slight layer of fat.

Do remember that, to human eyes, your Bichon's food intake will seem very small. Everything is proportionate, however, and even the smallest titbit will be a significant addition to the diet of your dog. You must be ever vigilant if your Bichon is to retain a waistline.

Neutering does not automatically mean that your Bichon will be overweight. Having an ovario-hysterectomy does slow down the body's rate of working, castration to a lesser extent, but it therefore means that your dog needs less food. I recommend cutting back a little on the amount of food fed a few weeks before neutering to accustom your Bichon to less food. If she looks a little underweight on the morning of the operation, it will help the

It is your responsibility to feed a well balanced diet to maintain the correct weight.

veterinary surgeon as well as giving her a little leeway weight-wise afterwards.

It is always harder to lose weight after neutering than before, because of this slowing in the body's inherent metabolic rate.

TEETH PROBLEMS

Eating food starts with the canine teeth gripping and killing prey in the wild, incisor teeth biting off pieces of food and the molar teeth chewing it. To be able to eat is vital for life, yet the actual health of the teeth is often over-looked: unhealthy teeth can predispose to disease, and not just by reducing the ability to eat. The presence of infection within the mouth can lead to bacteria entering the bloodstream and then filtering out at major organs, with the potential for serious consequences. That is not to forget that simply having dental pain can affect a dog's well-being, as anyone who has had tooth-ache will confirm.

Veterinary dentistry has made huge leaps in recent years, so that it no longer consists of extraction as the treatment of necessity.

Good dental health lies in the hands of the owner, starting from the moment the dog comes into your care. Just as we have taken on responsibility for feeding, so we have acquired the task of maintaining good dental and oral hygiene. In an ideal world, we should brush our dogs' teeth as regularly as our own. The Bichon puppy who finds having his teeth brushed is a huge game and an excuse to roll over and over on the ground requires loads of patience, twice a day.

There are alternative strategies ranging from dental chewsticks to specially formulated foods, but the main thing is to be aware of your dog's mouth. At least train your puppy to permit full examination of his teeth, which will not only ensure you are checking in his mouth regularly but also make your veterinary surgeon's job easier when there is a real need for your dog to 'open wide!'

We are fortunate that the Bichon suffers from relatively few breed inherited conditions.

INHERITED DISORDERS

Any individual, dog or human, may have an inherited disorder by virtue of genes acquired from the parents. This is significant not only for the health of that individual but also because of the potential for passing on the disorder to that individual's offspring and to subsequent generations, depending on the mode of inheritance.

There are control schemes in place for some inherited disorders. In the US, for example, the Canine Eye Registration Foundation (CERF) was set up by dog breeders concerned about heritable eye disease, and provides a database of dogs who have been examined by diplomates of the American College of Veterinary Ophthalmologists.

A few inherited conditions have been confirmed in the Bichon. These include the following.

CATARACTS

A cataract is a cloudiness of the lens of the eye. In the Bichon, this is a developmental cataract, which manifests from as young as six months of age through into late adulthood, in one or both eyes. The rate of progression is variable and can lead to blindness of the affected eye(s). Glaucoma may be a complicating factor. Inheritance appears to be as an autosomal recessive trait. It is controlled under Schedule B of the BVA/KC/ISDS Scheme (British Veterinary Association/Kennel Club/International Sheepdog Society) in the UK, CERF (Canine Eye Registration Foundation) in the UK.

CILIARY DYSKINESIA, PRIMARY

This anomaly of the upper respiratory tract first becomes apparent early in the life of affected puppies, which may be described as 'snorkelling'. There is a spectrum of signs, ranging from a yellow-green discharge from the nostrils and noisy rattling breathing through to those born with pneumonia who may die shortly after birth. An antibiotic course will often result in recovery, but this is usually only temporary, as the underlying problem remains. Recurrent bouts of sinusitis, bronchitis and pneumonia often become less frequent with age, and some affected individuals may eventually become free of illness by eighteen months of age.

The problem lies with the cilia, hair-like structures found in various places within the body. There are cilia on the mucus membranes lining the respiratory tract which are responsible for protecting the lungs from inhaled particles and pathogens by sweeping them away from the lungs to be coughed out of the body. In PCD, these cilia are deformed such that they cannot move in a co-ordinated fashion and the fluid accumulates in the airways, resulting in bronchitis and pneumonia.

Cilia are also found in the reproductive tract so infertility is not uncommon in Bichons with PCD. Rarely, a form of Hydrocephalus may also occur which, fortunately, tends not to cause problems.

Abnormal ciliary function during embryonic development while in the womb may be responsible for the occurrence of Situs Invertus Viscerum in 50 per cent of individuals with PCD. This is when the location of organs within the body has been reversed, ie as a mirror-image of

CORNEAL DYSTROPHY

The cornea is the transparent layer across the front of the eye. In the Bichon, the age at onset of Corneal Dystrophy is about two years. It affects the outer epithelial and underlying stromal layers of the cornea of both eyes, lipid being deposited in these layers and giving rise to grey or white opacities (marks). It progresses slowly, causing vision to become hazy and sometimes resulting in blindness. It is painless unless a corneal ulcer forms, which is rare with this form of Corneal Dystrophy. Inheritance is suspected in the Bichon.

the usual pattern.

PCD is an inherited defect which may be based on several genes. It seems to behave as an autosomal recessive because affected pups can be born to apparently healthy parents.

ENTROPION
This is an inrolling of the eyelids, usually of the medial or inner part of the lower eyelids. There are degrees of entropion, ranging from a slight inrolling to the more serious case requiring surgical correction because of the pain and damage to the surface of the eyeball (CERF).

HAEMOPHILIA A
Haemophilia is a common hereditary disorder of blood coagulation. It is inherited in a sex-linked recessive fashion. This means that the male is either affected or clear, whilst females can alternatively be carriers for the trait.

Haemophilia A arises from a deficiency of blood clotting Factor VIII. There are many ways in which haemophilia A can manifest, at worst as sudden death. There may be early indications, such as prolonged bleeding when the baby teeth are lost or unexpected bruising under the skin. A problem may not become apparent until after surgery such as routine neutering or an injury. Treatment will often require a blood transfusion.

HAEMOPHILIA B (CHRISTMAS DISEASE)
This is much less common than Haemophilia A and arises from a deficiency of the clotting factor IX.

HYPOTRICHOSIS, CONGENITAL
There is abnormal development or even a lack of hair follicles, resulting in a permanent absence of hair from birth or developing

within the first few weeks of life. The head, ears and abdomen are commonly affected, but, in more generalised cases, there may only be hair on top of the head and at the extremities of the tail and legs. Diagnosis is made on the basis of a skin biopsy.

Although the general health is not affected, the skin tends to darken and show seborrhoeic change, becoming greasy, scaly and smelly. Appropriate anti-seborrhoeic shampoos may therefore be very helpful. Care must be taken to avoid sunburn, to which pale skin is susceptible, and also frostbite.

LEGGE-CALVE-PERTHES DISEASE

Also called Legge-Perthes disease, the problem is more accurately described as an avascular necrosis of the femoral head, meaning the ball of the thigh bone dies. This results in severe pain and lameness, which become apparent during the first year of life.

Surgery can be quite effective. Early diagnosis and treatment through pain relief and resting of the affected back-leg in a sling may avoid the need for surgical intervention.

PATELLAR LUXATION

This is the condition that I point out to my children when I spot a dog walking along the road, giving a little hop for a few steps every now and again.

The patella or kneecap is supposed to glide within a groove on the front aspect of the thigh bone (femur) during bending and straightening of the knee joint. The term 'patellar luxation' refers to the situation whereby the kneecap slips out of position, locking the knee or stifle so that it will not bend and causing the characteristic hopping steps until the patella slips back into its position over the stifle joint. If the patella is unstable but not actually slipping out of the joint, then the term 'patellar subluxation' is used.

There are various underlying factors. The problem may be only intermittent, the patella returning to its usual position of its own accord, or a more constant feature requiring manual manipulation to restore normal joint anatomy. It predisposes to degenerative joint disease (arthritis). Corrective surgery can be performed with variable results.

PATENT DUCTUS ARTERIOSUS

This is a common congenital abnormality in the canine population. It is inherited in a polygenic fashion in the Bichon, with females being predisposed. The ductus arteriosus is a normal feature of the fetus, running from the pulmonary artery to the descending aorta and enabling most of the blood to bypass the lungs during life in the womb; the lungs are not needed for respiration but simply need enough blood for their own development. With the pup's first breath, and by the eighth

It is essential that all breeding stock is thoroughly health checked as this helps to eliminate inherited disorders from bloodlines.

day of life, this shunt should seal and no longer be patent, so that all the blood leaving the right side of the heart is taken to the lungs and thence back to the left side of the heart.

Persistence of the ductus arteriosus adversely affects the cardiovascular system and will ultimately result in heart failure. The characteristic continuous heart murmur may also be felt with the fingers across the chest wall as a so-called 'thrill'. Early diagnosis is essential before clinical signs have developed, enabling surgical intervention in most, but not all, cases.

PORTO-SYSTEMIC SHUNT

This is a rare congenital condition where there are blood vessels bypassing the liver. The liver has a wide range of important roles within the body, including the removal and processing of toxins from the blood – if it is not receiving all the blood flow, it cannot function effectively. This results in the development of liver disease at a young age or may only become apparent later in life.

In small breeds such as the Bichon, the shunting vessels tend to occur outside the liver and may therefore be amenable to surgery. Rarely, microvascular shunts may exist, giving rise to less marked illness.

There is some evidence from analysis of pedigrees for inheritance of this condition in the Bichon.

UROLITHIASIS

Urolithiasis is the presence of stones or excessive amounts of crystals within the urinary tract, in the dog most commonly in the bladder. They irritate the lining of the urinary tract, resulting in pain and blood in the urine. They may predispose to a secondary bacterial infection. In some instances, they may actually partially or totally block the outflow of urine, which requires emergency treatment.

Different biochemical types of uroliths have been recognised. Some surveys of Bichons have found a higher than expected incidence of various types of urolithiasis in this breed.

WHITE DOG SHAKER SYNDROME, SHAKER DOG DISEASE

This is more common in the Maltese, a cousin of the Bichon. Alternative names include Little White Shakers Syndrome, Ideopathic Tremor Syndrome and Acquired Tremor in young adult dogs.

It tends to have an acute onset in the young dog aged six months to three years, progressively worsening over a short period of one to three days before stabilising until treatment is initiated. The tremor is generalised and shows a wide spectrum from mild shaking to such a severe tremor that it is difficult for the affected individual to walk. The tremor is described as an intention tremor, meaning that it is worse when attempting a movement or when excited, but reduces in severity or even disappears when relaxed. There may be a head tilt, and the eyes may make quick random movements.

Affected individuals usually respond well and the tremor may resolve totally when given corticosteroids and/or a benzodiazepine such as diazepam. Long-term, low-dose therapy may be needed in order to avoid a return of the signs.

COMPLEMENTARY THERAPIES

Just as for human health, I believe there is a place for alternative therapies alongside and complementing orthodox treatment under the supervision of a veterinary surgeon. That is why 'complementary therapies' is a better name.

Because animals do not have a choice, there are measures in place to safeguard their wellbeing and welfare. All manipulative treatment must be under the direction of a veterinary surgeon who has examined the patient

Increasingly owners are turning to complementary therapies to back up conventional treatment.

and diagnosed the condition which she or he feels needs that form of treatment. This covers physiotherapy, chiropractic, osteopathy and swimming therapy. For example, dogs with arthritis who cannot exercise as freely as they were accustomed will enjoy the sensation of controlled non-weight-bearing exercise in water, and benefit with improved muscling and overall fitness.

All other complementary therapies such as acupuncture, homoeopathy and aromatherapy can only be carried out by veterinary surgeons who have been trained in that particular field. Acupuncture is mainly used in dog for pain relief, often to good effect. The needles look more alarming to the owner, but they are very fine and are well tolerated by most canine patients. Speaking personally, superficial needling is not unpleasant and does help with pain relief.

Homoeopathy has had a mixed press in recent years. It is based on the concept of treating like with like. Additionally, a homoeopathic remedy is said to become more powerful the more it is diluted.

CONCLUSION
As the owner of a Bichon, you are responsible for his care and health. Not only must you make decisions on his behalf, you are also responsible for establishing a

lifestyle for him that will ensure he leads a long and happy life.

Diet plays as important a part in the dog's overall health as exercise, for example. Nutritional manipulation has a long history. Formulation of animal feedstuffs is aimed at optimising production from, for example, dairy cattle. For the domestic dog, it is only in recent years that the need has been recognised for changing the diet to suit the dog as he grows, matures and then enters his twilight years. So-called life-stage diets try to match the nutritional needs of the dog as he progresses through life.

An adult dog food will suit the Bichon living a standard family life. There are also foods for those Bichons tactfully termed as obese-prone, such as those who have been neutered or are less active than others, or simply like their food. Do remember, though, that ultimately you are in control of your Bichon's diet, unless he is able to profit from scavenging!

On the other hand, prescription diets are, of necessity, fed under the supervision of a veterinary surgeon because each is formulated to meet the very specific needs of particular health conditions. Should a prescription diet be fed to a healthy dog, or

With good care and management, your Bichon should live a long, happy and healthy life.

to a dog with a different illness, there could be adverse effects.

It is important to remember that your Bichon has no choice. As his owner, you are responsible for any decision made so it must be as informed a decision as

possible. Always speak to your veterinary surgeon if you have any worries about your Bichon. He is not just a dog: he will have become a definite member of the family from the moment you brought him home.

THE CONTRIBUTORS

THE EDITOR:
CHRIS WYATT (BOBANDER)

Chris Wyatt has been involved with all aspects of the Bichon Frisé since 1982. This includes a highly successful show career making up ten Bobander UK Champions with all but one being home bred. As a Championship show judge Chris awards Challenge Certificates in Bichons in the UK, but has also judged Bichons in New Zealand, Norway, Sweden and Ireland. For several years Chris has written the breed notes for the weekly publication *Dog World*.
See Chapter One: Introducing the Bichon Frisé and Chapter Seven: The Perfect Bichon Frisé.

ELIZABETH KELMAN JACK (SHOOLTERS)

Although not being brought up with dogs, Elizabeth has been involved with them for the last 56 years, first with Working, Utility and Hounds, then in 1977 she bought her first Bichon Frisé dog. This was followed a year later by his half sister who became her foundation bitch under the Shoolters affix.

Elizabeth is one of the longest standing members of the Bichon Frisé Club of Great Britain and has awarded KC Challenge Certificates in the breed since 1991. In 2002 she had the honour to be elected president of the SBFBA (Southern Bichon Frisé Breeders Association), a position she holds today.

Although no longer breeding, she is still deeply involved with the Bichon and currently contributse to the breed notes for one of the weekly dog papers.
See Chapter Two: The First Bichon Frisé.

DAWN RUSSELL (RUSMAR)

Dawn Russell first became involved in Bichons in 1980, after looking after one for a friend. This Bichon, Katie, became Dawn's foundation bitch. Since then, through careful and selective breeding Dawn has managed to produce 10 Champions in the UK and several overseas Champions including Best in Show winners in New Zealand and Australia. Dawn also breeds and shows Afghan Hounds, the two breeds living happily alongside one another.

Dawn awards the Challenge Certificates in both Bichon Frisé and Afghan Hounds, and judges most other breeds at Open Show level.
See Chapter Three: A Bichon for your Lifestyle. Chapter Five: the Best of Care.

PAULINE JOHNS (MANOIR)

Pauline bought her first Bichon in 1990. Her daughter, then aged ten, started to show him and that was the beginning of Pauline's involvement in the show world. She bred her first litter in 1996 and by 1999 produced the first of her 14 Champions; seven in the UK and seven overseas. To date, 16 of her home-bred Bichons have gained stud book status. She judges the Toy Group at Open shows and Bichons at Championship level. She has attended over 30 seminars maintaining her avid interest in Bichons.
See Chapter Four: The New Arrival.

CAROLINE BOWMAN DIPAVN(SURGICAL), VN, MBNA (CARREGIS)

Caroline qualified as a Veterinary Nurse in 1999 having studied at various referral Veterinary Hospitals and The Royal Veterinary College, London. On completion of her qualification she worked in numerous referral Veterinary Hospitals and General Practices whilst completing further training to gain The Diploma in Advanced Veterinary Nursing - Surgical in 2002. She continued to work in referral hospitals before moving to Bedfordshire where she now lives with her partner, combining part time work at a Small Animal General Practice with looking after their two young children. Her Carregis affix is owned jointly with her mother Carol, who exhibits the Bichons with husband Graham. They have produced three Carregis Bichon Champions to date.
See Chapter Five: The Best Of Care.

JULIA BARNES

Julia has owned and trained a number of different dog breed, and has also worked as a puppy socialiser for Dogs for the Disabled. A former journalist, she has written many books, including several on dog training and behaviour. Julia is indebted to Chris Wyatt for her specialist knowledge about training Bichon Frisé.
See Chapter Six: Training and Socialisation.

ALISON LOGAN MA VetMB MRCVS

Alison qualified as a veterinary surgeon from Cambridge University in 1989, having been brought up surrounded by all manner of animals and birds in the north Essex countryside. She has been in practice in her home town ever since, living with her husband, two children and Labrador Retriever Pippin.

She contributes on a regular basis to *Veterinary Times, Veterinary Nurse Times, Dogs Today, Cat World* and *Pet Patter*, the PetPlan newsletter. In 1995, Alison won the Univet Literary Award with an article on Cushing's Disease, and she won it again (as the Vetoquinol Literary Award) in 2002, writing about common conditions in the Shar-Pei.
See Chapter Eight: Happy and Healthy.

USEFUL ADDRESSES

KENNEL & BREED CLUBS

UK
The Kennel Club
1-5 Clarges Street, London, W1J 8AB
Tel: 0870 606 6750
Fax: 0207 518 1058
Web: www.the-kennel-club.org.uk

To obtain up-to-date contact information for the following breed clubs, contact the Kennel Club:
• Bichon Frisé Club of Great Britain
• Northern and Midland Bichon Frisé Club
• Southern Bichon Frisé Breeders Association

USA
American Kennel Club (AKC)
5580 Centerview Drive,
Raleigh, NC 27606, USA.
Tel: 919 233 9767
Fax: 919 233 3627
Email: info@akc.org
Web: www.akc.org

United Kennel Club (UKC)
100 E Kilgore Rd, Kalamazoo,
MI 49002-5584, USA.
Tel: 269 343 9020
Fax: 269 343 7037
Web:www.ukcdogs.com/

The Bichon Frise Club of America, Inc.
Web: http://www.bichon.org/

For contact details of regional clubs, please contact The Bichon Frisé Club of America.

AUSTRALIA
Australian National Kennel Council (ANKC)
The Australian National Kennel Council is the administrative body for pure breed canine affairs in Australia. It does not, however, deal directly with dog exhibitors, breeders or judges. For information pertaining to breeders, clubs or shows, please contact the relevant State or Territory Controlling Body.

Dogs Australian Capital Territory
PO Box 815, Dickson ACT 2602
Tel: (02) 6241 4404
Fax: (02) 6241 1129
Email: administrator@dogsact.org.au
Web: www.dogsact.org.au

Dogs New South Wales
PO Box 632, St Marys, NSW 1790
Tel: (02) 9834 3022 or 1300 728 022 (NSW Only)
Fax: (02) 9834 3872
Email: info@dogsnsw.org.au
Web: www.dogsnsw.org.au

Dogs Northern Territory
PO Box 37521, Winnellie NT 0821
Tel: (08) 8984 3570

Fax: (08) 8984 3409
Email: admin@dogsnt.com.au
Web: www.dogsnt.com.au

Dogs Queensland
PO Box 495, Fortitude Valley Qld 4006
Tel: (07) 3252 2661
Fax: (07) 3252 3864
Email: info@dogsqueensland.org.au
Web: www.dogsqueensland.org.au

Dogs South Australia
PO Box 844
Prospect East SA 5082
Tel: (08) 8349 4797
Fax: (08) 8262 5751
Email: info@dogssa.com.au
Web: www.dogssa.com.au

Tasmanian Canine Association Inc
The Rothman Building
PO Box 116
Glenorchy Tas 7010
Tel: (03) 6272 9443
Fax: (03) 6273 0844
Email: tca@iprimus.com.au
Web: www.tasdogs.com

Dogs Victoria
Locked Bag K9
Cranbourne VIC 3977
Tel: (03) 9788 2500
Fax: (03) 9788 2599
Email: office@dogsvictoria.org.au
Web: www.dogsvictoria.org.au

Dogs Western Australia
PO Box 1404
Canning Vale WA 6970
Tel: (08) 9455 1188
Fax: (08) 9455 1190
Email: k9@dogswest.com
Web: www.dogswest.com

INTERNATIONAL
Fédération Cynologique Internationalé (FCI)/World Canine Organisation
Place Albert 1er, 13, B-6530 Thuin,
Belgium.
Tel: +32 71 59.12.38
Fax: +32 71 59.22.29
Web: www.fci.be/

TRAINING AND BEHAVIOUR

UK
Association of Pet Dog Trainers
PO Box 17, Kempsford, GL7 4WZ
Telephone: 01285 810811
Email: APDToffice@aol.com
Web: http://www.apdt.co.uk

Association of Pet Behaviour Counsellors
PO BOX 46, Worcester, WR8 9YS

Telephone: 01386 751151
Fax: 01386 750743
Email: info@apbc.org.uk
Web: http://www.apbc.org.uk/

USA
Association of Pet Dog Trainers
101 North Main Street, Suite 610
Greenville, SC 29601, USA.
Tel: 1 800 738 3647
Email: information@apdt.com
Web: www.apdt.com/

American College of Veterinary Behaviorists
College of Veterinary Medicine, 4474 Tamu, Texas A&M University
College Station, Texas 77843-4474
Web: http://dacvb.org/

American Veterinary Society of Animal Behavior
Web: www.avsabonline.org/

AUSTRALIA
APDT Australia Inc
PO Box 3122, Bankstown Square, NSW 2200,
Email: secretary@apdt.com.au
Web: www.apdt.com.au

Canine Behaviour
For details of regional behvaiourists, contact the relevant State or Territory Controlling Body.

ACTIVITIES

UK
Agility Club
http://www.agilityclub.co.uk/

British Flyball Association
PO Box 990, Doncaster, DN1 9FY
Telephone: 01628 829623
Email: secretary@flyball.org.uk
Web: http://www.flyball.org.uk/

USA
North American Dog Agility Council
P.O. Box 1206, Colbert,
OK 74733, USA.
Web: www.nadac.com/

North American Flyball Association, Inc.
1333 West Devon Avenue, #512
Chicago, IL 60660
Tel/Fax: 800 318 6312
Email: flyball@flyball.org
Web: www.flyball.org/

AUSTRALIA
Agility Dog Association of Australia
ADAA Secretary, PO Box 2212,
Gailes, QLD 4300, Australia.
Tel: 0423 138 914
Email: admin@adaa.com.au
Web: www.adaa.com.au/

NADAC Australia (North American Dog Agility Council - Australian Division)
12 Wellman Street, Box Hill South, Victoria 3128, Australia.
Email: shirlene@nadacaustralia.com
Web: www.nadacaustralia.com/

Australian Flyball Association
PO Box 4179, Pitt Town, NSW 2756
Tel: 0407 337 939
Email: info@flyball.org.au
Web: www.flyball.org.au/

INTERNATIONAL

World Canine Freestyle Organisation
P.O. Box 350122, Brooklyn, NY 11235-2525, USA
Tel: (718) 332-8336
Fax: (718) 646-2686
Email: wcfodogs@aol.com
Web: www.worldcaninefreestyle.org

HEALTH

UK
Alternative Veterinary Medicine Centre
Chinham House, Stanford in the Vale, Oxfordshire, SN7 8NQ
Tel: 01367 710324
Fax: 01367 718243
Web: www.alternativevet.org/

British Small Animal Veterinary Association
Woodrow House, 1 Telford Way, Waterwells Business Park, Quedgeley, Gloucestershire, GL2 2AB
Tel: 01452 726700
Fax: 01452 726701
Email: customerservices@bsava.com
Web: http://www.bsava.com/

Royal College of Veterinary Surgeons
Belgravia House, 62-64 Horseferry Road, London, SW1P 2AF
Tel: 0207 222 2001
Fax: 0207 222 2004
Email: admin@rcvs.org.uk
Web: www.rcvs.org.uk

USA
American Holistic Veterinary Medical Association
2218 Old Emmorton Road
Bel Air, MD 21015
Tel: 410 569 0795
Fax 410 569 2346
Email: office@ahvma.org
Web: www.ahvma.org/

American Veterinary Medical Association
1931 North Meacham Road, Suite 100, Schaumburg, IL 60173-4360, USA.
Tel: 800 248 2862
Fax: 847 925 1329
Web: www.avma.org

American College of Veterinary Surgeons
19785 Crystal Rock Dr, Suite 305
Germantown, MD 20874, USA.
Tel: 301 916 0200
Toll Free: 877 217 2287
Fax: 301 916 2287
Email: acvs@acvs.org
Web: www.acvs.org/

AUSTRALIA
Australian Holistic Vets
Web: www.ahv.com.au/

Australian Small Animal Veterinary Association
40/6 Herbert Street, St Leonards, NSW 2065, Australia.
Tel: 02 9131 5090
Fax: 02 9437 9068
Email: asava@ava.com.au
Web: www.asava.com.au

Australian Veterinary Association
Unit 40, 6 Herbert Street, St Leonards, NSW 2065, Australia.
Tel: 02 9431 5000
Fax: 02 9437 9068
Web: www.ava.com.au

Australian College Veterinary Scientists
Building 3, Garden City Office Park, 2404 Logan Road, Eight Mile Plains, Queensland 4113, Australia.
Tel: 07 3423 2016
Fax: 07 3423 2977
Email: admin@acvs.org.au
Web: http://acvsc.org.au

ASSISTANCE DOGS

UK
Canine Partners
Mill Lane, Heyshott, Midhurst, GU29 0ED
Tel: 08456 580480
Fax: 08456 580481
Web: www.caninepartners.co.uk

Dogs for the Disabled
The Frances Hay Centre, Blacklocks Hill, Banbury, Oxon, OX17 2BS
Tel: 01295 252600
Web: www.dogsforthedisabled.org

Guide Dogs for the Blind Association
Burghfield Common, Reading, RG7 3YG
Tel: 01189 835555
Fax: 01189 835433
Web: www.guidedogs.org.uk/

Hearing Dogs for Deaf People
The Grange, Wycombe Road, Saunderton, Princes Risborough, Bucks, HP27 9NS
Tel: 01844 348100
Fax: 01844 348101
Web: www.hearingdogs.org.uk

Pets as Therapy
14a High Street, Wendover, Aylesbury, Bucks. HP22 6EA.
Tel: 01845 345445
Fax: 01845 550236
Web: http://www.petsastherapy.org/

Support Dogs
21 Jessops Riverside, Brightside Lane, Sheffield, S9 2RX
Tel: 01142 617800
Fax: 01142 617555
Email: supportdogs@btconnect.com
Web: www.support-dogs.org.uk

USA
Therapy Dogs International
88 Bartley Road, Flanders, NJ 07836,.
Tel: 973 252 9800
Fax: 973 252 7171
Web: www.tdi-dog.o

Therapy Dogs Inc.
P.O. Box 20227, Cheyenne, WY 82003.
Tel: 307 432 0272.
Fax: 307-638-2079
Web: www.therapydogs.com

Delta Society - Pet Partners
875 124th Ave NE, Suite 101, Bellevue, WA 98005 USA.
Email: info@DeltaSociety.org
Web: www.deltasociety.org

Comfort Caring Canines
8135 Lare Street, Philadelphia, PA 19128.
Email: ccc@comfortcaringcanines.org
Web: www.comfortcaringcanines.org/

AUSTRALIA
AWARE Dogs Australia, Inc
PO Box 883, Kuranda, Queensland, 488..
Tel: 07 4093 8152
Web: www.awaredogs.org.au/

Delta Society — Therapy Dogs
Web: www.deltasociety.com.au